Becoming a
NURSE

Becoming a
NURSE

CONTRA COSTA COUNTY
JUVENILE HALL LIBRARY

LEARNINGEXPRESS®

NEW YORK

Library of Congress Cataloging-in-Publication Data:
Becoming a nurse.—1st ed.
    p. ; cm.
  ISBN 978-1-57685-692-5
    1. Nursing—Vocational guidance.   I. LearningExpress (Organization)
    [DNLM: 1. Nursing.   2. Career Choice.   3. Vocational Guidance.   WY 16
    B3975 2009]
    RT82.B43 2009
    610.7306'9—dc22

                                                          2009003796

Printed in the United States of America

9 8 7 6 5 4 3 2 1

First Edition

ISBN 978-1-57685-692-5

Regarding the Information in This Book

Every effort has been made to ensure the accuracy of directory information up until press
time. However, phone numbers and/or addresses are subject to change. Please contact the
respective organization for the most recent information.

For more information or to place an order, contact LearningExpress at:
  2 Rector Street
  26th Floor
  New York, NY 10006

Or visit us at:
  www.learnatest.com

Contents

Acknowledgments

THE AUTHOR would like to thank the following people for their assistance with this book:

Jennifer Pollock, Senior Editor, for her support and guidance throughout this project.

The contributors: nursing students from the Decker School of Nursing at Binghamton University in New York, the University of Scranton in Pennsylvania, and East Stroudsburg University in Pennsylvania; and practicing nurses in New York and Pennsylvania:

Tina Abbate

Laura Benjamin

Jessica Beyer

Jahaira Capellan

Amy Carbone

Katie Cannizzo

Lisa Daly

Rajae Elkirami

Kathryn Ericksen

Mike Evans

Milt Evans

Ashley French

Marybeth Gabriel

John Gao

Laura Garrison
Lindsay Giordano
Samantha Guy
Christina Haggerty
Valarie Hermann
Alexandra Karlgut
Krista Lee Kelsey
Katrina Kruckzo
Olivia Kurtoglu
Essie Lee
Katherine Levis
Mandy Lorenz
Mary Kate McFarland
Monica Mazurowski
Ashley Panaro
Terri Parkin
Jacquelynn Pasamba
Kelly Peterson
Andrea Randrup

Paige Reynolds
Sara Rieger
Isabel Roitman
Howie Romans
Scott Rosman
Nicole Rouhana
Nicole Russo
Jolynn Sannicandro
Jerome Scarpati
Jessica Schmoyer
Neil Smartschan
Michele Summers
Kelly Thompson-Brazill
Nicole Trama
Caitlin Van Brunt
Krista Wachendorfer
Rosemary Welte
Faye Zhong

A special thanks goes to contributors Kelly Thompson-Brazill and Monica Mazurowski for their extended contributions.

This book is dedicated to nursing students everywhere for the committed care you give your clients and the ongoing inspiration you give to your teachers.

Introduction

THINKING ABOUT becoming a nurse? Maybe your father is an emergency room nurse, and you're interested in knowing more about other nursing specialties before you graduate high school and plan for your career. Or, perhaps you're a newly divorced single parent who wants to explore nursing as an option to better your life and those of your children. You may even be a recent retiree or at midlife and ready for a complete change from working a desk or the sales floor. Regardless of your rationale or age, nursing may be the career for you. You can become a practical nurse (PN) through a vocational program or a registered nurse (RN) via a college degree. If you already have a degree, you can complete an accelerated program, finishing your BSN (bachelor's degree in nursing) in as little as 12 months. You can choose to spend your career working in a hospital or physician's office, or you can continue your education and become an advance practice nurse, nurse educator, or nurse administrator, or you can chose from a long list of options to make your nursing career work for you.

KELLY'S STORY

Kelly Thompson-Brazill, MSN, ACNP, RN, CCRN
Nurse Practitioner, Cardiothoracic Surgery
Wake Med Health & Hospitals, Raleigh Campus

When I was seventeen, I was diagnosed with advanced stage Hodgkin's lymphoma. I spent eight months on chemotherapy. I had an excellent oncologist and a wonderful team of nurses caring for me. I went into remission relatively quickly, but I spent the next two years reconciling what I was "supposed" to do with what I actually wanted to do with my life. While I was receiving chemo, my pediatrician was pushing me toward medical school. My mother nudged me toward pharmacy school. So when I entered the University of Scranton, I dutifully majored in biology. I hated it.

Still reconciling emotions of surviving cancer and my parents' recent divorce, I had trouble concentrating on my studies. I spiraled into a major depression during my first semester freshman year. Now on academic probation and with my scholarships on the line, I decided I needed to find a new major, but I wasn't sure which I should choose, so I took a semester of general liberal arts classes to help me figure it out. My depression abated and my grades improved.

During that summer, I began working as a registration clerk at the emergency department of a very small hospital. I was in awe of a nurse named, Lisa. Lisa was a fairly new nurse, but she knew a lot and always interacted so well with the patients. I really admired her. I enjoyed watching her perform skills and comfort patients and their families, just as I had with my former oncology nurses. One day, I finally realized that the people I looked up to the most, who helped me recover both physically and emotionally from cancer, weren't physicians, they were nurses.

As a result, I applied to the nursing program at my university. Given my recent academic probation, I met with the program chair to discuss my career plans and explain why a former straight-A student had such poor grades. She agreed to let me into the nursing major. I was thrilled. I spent the next four years learning biology, chemistry, pharmacology, and nursing theory. I fell in love with critical care. I made great friends. I had a wonderful professor who encouraged me to write my first article, which was about early detection of Hodgkin's disease. It was published while I was still in college. Because of her, I continue writing today.

After graduating, I worked in a cardiothoracic intensive care unit. I wanted to learn as much as possible, so I decided to get my master's degree. My husband (then fiancé) and I moved to North Carolina and I enrolled in the nurse practitioner program at Duke University. While at Duke, I had great didactic classes and clinical rotations. I finished my acute care nurse practitioner residency in trauma and surgical critical care at Pitt County Memorial Hospital, a large teaching and level-1 trauma hospital in Greenville, North Carolina. I took a nurse practitioner position with the program after finishing my residency.

My colleagues and I spent several years building the advanced-level practitioner program from the ground up. We started managing patients on the floors and soon worked our way up to managing complex poly-trauma and other critically ill surgical patients. We even began performing invasive procedures such as intubations, chest tube insertions, and arterial line, central line and pulmonary artery catheter placements. While at Pitt, I participated in a number of quality improvement measures. I received an evidence-based practice grant from the American Association of Critical Care Nurses (AACN) to evaluate our program, "The Impact of a Clinical Management Guideline on the Prevention of Ventilator Associated Pneumonia (VAP)." This was a huge undertaking. Ultimately, we reduced VAP rates by approximately 29% in our trauma population. The measure was so successful that it was adopted by all of the adult intensive care units at our institution.

Later, I took the position of lead advanced level practitioner for the trauma program. This was an excellent learning experience. Not only did I have administrative and clinical functions, but I was also able to participate in program development. Throughout my time with the hospital, I participated on national work groups for AACN and reviewed manuscripts for two nursing journals.

Within the last year, I have left trauma and returned to cardiothoracic surgery as a nurse practitioner at a tertiary cardiac referral center in Raleigh. This has allowed me to spend more time with my three-year-old daughter. I have also had more opportunities to continue teaching critical care and trauma courses for nurses throughout the country and participate on national committees for the Society of Critical Care Medicine.

People are frequently astounded that someone my age (I'm in my early thirties) could have done so much in nursing so soon. When I hear this I often think of a quote inscribed on a wall at the University of Scranton:

> "Of those to whom much is given, much is expected."

Truthfully, it's not hard to accomplish a lot when you are doing something you love. I am passionate about nursing and improving patient care. This is what I was meant to do. And I am very thankful for the many excellent mentors who have guided me on my journey.

Nursing is one of the top ten occupations expected to offer the largest number of new jobs in the coming years. Nurses are in such high demand that hardly a week goes by without schools receiving recruitment letters from hospitals, outpatient facilities, nursing homes, prisons, and healthcare employment agencies. This book was designed to help you begin and expand your nursing career.

Chapter 1: The Department of Labor lists registered nursing as a top occupation for job growth through at least the next decade. But don't consider nursing just for the tangible benefits. Nurses blend art and science to care for others, creating a career path that is the perfect blend of high touch and high tech. Chapter 1 introduces you to the levels of nursing, the nursing process, standards of nursing practice, ethical and legal issues, and the nurse-client partnership.

Chapter 2: One nurse's pro is another's con. Nursing is such a versatile profession that there's something in it for almost anyone, but nursing isn't for everyone. This chapter weighs the positive and negative features of nursing, focusing on the nursing experience, which gives you a skill-by-skill description of basic nursing functions. After considering all the pros and cons, take the suitability test to see if nursing is right for you.

Chapter 3: The first step toward becoming a nurse is selecting the educational program that's right for you. This chapter describes the differences between the educational requirements for practical and registered nurses, including the various registered nursing programs. You'll learn about nursing courses, admission requirements, costs, financial aid, and ROTC. It also contains valuable educational options for people who already have a degree and who want to fast-track into nursing.

Chapter 4: Graduate education (master's and doctoral degrees) enable nurses to assume advanced roles in education, administration, research, and clinical practice. This chapter explains the functions and educational require-ments for these roles, and introduces you to nursing doctoral education.

Chapter 5: All nurses need to be licensed, and this chapter explains the process from preparation to becoming a licensed nurse. Since nursing re-quires ongoing learning, this chapter also introduces you to continuing edu-cation and certification.

Chapter 6: A career in nursing can take you along many different paths. There is a nursing specialty for every medical specialty, and more. This chapter explores the majority of nursing specialties, including links to their organizations and certification information. It also helps you with your job hunt, especially addressing resume writing and interviewing.

Chapter 7: The final chapter wraps things up with what it means to be a nurse. Nursing students and nurses from a variety of backgrounds share their stories of what nursing means to them. They share the good and the bad, each in his or her own style. Some of the students are young adults fresh out of high school; others are beginning second careers as nurses. Many share how to juggle college life with the hectic pace of nursing, while others shed light on what it's like to split your life between nursing, family, and work. Seasoned nurses talk about advanced practice experiences and reminisce about their first days on the job. All of these men and women have one thing in common, their love of nursing. No matter how difficult their journey, they all cherish their ability to make a difference in the lives of others.

CHAPTER one

THE DEPARTMENT of Labor lists registered nursing as a top occupation for job growth through at least the next decade. Employment of registered nurses (RNs) is expected to grow much faster than the average for all occupations through 2016, resulting in 587,000 new jobs, among the largest number of new jobs for any occupation. Add to this the fact that hundreds of thousands of job openings will result from the need to replace experienced nurses who leave the occupation, and you have the makings of a recession-resistant career with a median annual earning rate of $57,280.

Projected employment for licensed practical nurses (LPNs, also called licensed vocational nurses [LVNs] in some states) also looks very promising, with a growth rate of 14% from 2006 to 2016 and a median annual earning rate of $36,550. LPNs can expect the best job opportunities to occur in nursing care facilities and home healthcare services, as applicants for jobs in hospitals may face competition.

But don't consider nursing just for the tangible benefits. Nurses blend art and science to care for others, creating a career path that is the perfect blend of high touch and high tech. As a nurse, you can make a difference in people's lives: when a baby takes her first breath and when an elder takes his last; when acute illness suddenly strikes and when chronic disease continuously takes its toll; and when a person threatens to take their life or that of another. No other profession offers the opportunities to do so much for so many, especially for oneself.

WHAT IS NURSING?

The word *nursing* conjures up a vast array of images. Some may think of the winged white caps, starched white uniforms, opaque white stockings, and polished white oxfords of yesteryear. Others may envision crusty battle-axes or soap opera kittens frequently portrayed in the media. But most people view nursing for what it is, a respected group of well-educated, hard-working and caring women and men who get people through some of the most difficult times of their lives.

The American Nurses Association defines nursing as: "the protection, promotion, and optimization of health and abilities, prevention of illness and injury, alleviation of suffering through the diagnosis and treatment of human response, and advocacy in the care of individuals, families, communities, and populations." Therefore, nursing is a career that enables you to help people maintain or regain their optimal health, while at the same time offering you numerous avenues for flexibility and growth over the course of your career.

How does this differ from other healthcare professions? Nursing focuses on the client's response to actual or potential health problems. Nursing is holistic, centering on the whole person, not just the person's presenting health problem. Nurses use a blend of psychology and physiology to build on their understanding of the health and illness processes to promote the restoration and maintenance of health.

Florence Nightingale described nursing as having "charge of the personal health of somebody . . . and what nursing has to do . . . is to put the patient in the best condition for nature to act upon him." Modern definitions of nursing define it as an art and science concentrating on quality of life as defined by the client. Nursing is concerned about the quality of health and functioning, as well as quality of living and dying, lived experience, and the universal lived experiences of health. Nursing focuses on health promotion and maintenance, as well as curative, restorative, supportive, and terminal care to individuals, families, and groups, taking into consideration the factors that influence them in the total environment.

The art of nursing practice is grounded in scientific principles. The science of nursing involves the study of relationships among nurses, clients, and their environments within the context of healthcare. It is essential to the discipline, generating theory and knowledge that support and advance healthcare. While nursing has incorporated theories from other disciplinary sources, such as systems, human needs, change, decision-making, and problem-solving theories, nursing has also developed its own conceptual models and theories. Nightingale introduced nursing theory in her book, *Notes on Nursing: What it is and What it is Not*, when she conceptualized the nurse's role as manipulating the environment to facilitate the reparative process by attending to light, ventilation, noise, cleanliness, and diet. Her framework is still evident in nursing today. While nursing theories have become more sophisticated, they all share four central and interconnected concepts: person, environment, health, and nursing.

Person or client refers to individuals, families, groups, communities, and populations who are holistic entities interacting with the environment. Persons have common basic needs and inherent dignity and self-worth. Persons/clients are active partners in their healthcare and represent diversity in relation to age, gender, ethnicity, race, religion, socioeconomic status, values, lifestyle, and functional ability level. The *environment* is multidimensional with internal and external conditions, influences, and phenomena. The environment is both reciprocal and complementary to the person, interacting within interrelated biological, physical, social, economic, and political context. Seen as fluid and dynamic, *health* is highly sensitive to the client's ability to adjust and adapt to the environment. The environment influences beliefs and health and consists of physical, psychological, biological, social, spiritual, and cultural components. Through complex adaptation processes, the health of the person varies from high-level wellness to illness and death. The goal is optimum wellness. Nursing believes that health is the responsibility of all and that all people have the right to healthcare. *Nursing* is a discipline and practice profession that serves to diagnose and treat human responses to actual or potential health problems. Utilizing the principles of evidence-based practice, nursing forms a therapeutic alliance and a professional partnership that holistically seeks to promote, protect, and restore health patterns for clients through time and across settings.

Depending on their level, practice type, and/or employment setting, nurses fulfill a number of different roles, which primarily include:

Care provider: Nurses combine the art of caring and the science of nursing to meet the holistic needs of individuals, families, communities, and populations through collaboration with other health professionals.

Advocate: Nurses identify the needs and goals of clients, while assisting them in making informed decisions. Nurses also promote human dignity, respect diversity, and protect the ethical and legal rights of clients.

Educator: Nurses use therapeutic communication skills to assess, plan, implement, and evaluate client learning. They share information formally and informally and act as consultants to promote, restore, and maintain health.

Researcher: Nurses use and participate in nursing research to increase knowledge in nursing and utilize evidence-based practice to improve client care.

Leader: Nurses demonstrate an ability to communicate effectively, use critical thinking skills, coordinate cost-effective nursing care, and provide case management. They delegate care, guide and direct others, and collaborate with interdisciplinary healthcare teams.

LEVELS OF NURSING

When it comes to planning a nursing career, few factors are more confusing than the different levels of nursing: practical nursing, registered nursing, and advanced practice nursing.

Practical Nurses

Licensed practical nurses (LPN), also called licensed vocational nurses (LVN) in some states, care for patients under the direction of physicians and registered nurses. Most are generalists, working in all areas of healthcare, but some work in specialized settings. According to the Bureau of Labor Statistics, LPNs held about 749,000 jobs in 2006, with about 26% of LPNs working in hospitals, 26% in nursing care facilities, and 12% in physician offices. Others worked for home healthcare services; employment services; residential care facilities; community care facilities for the elderly; outpatient care centers; and federal, state, and local government agencies. About 19% of LPNs worked part-time.

LPNs in the workforce tend to fit in one of three categories: (1) those who had no formal education and who completed state-approved courses that qualified them to become licensed; (2) those who were licensed through "grandfathering" (exempt from new licensure rules); and (3) those who graduated from approved schools and have passed a licensure examination. In most states, those wishing to become LPNs today must graduate from an approved practical nurse program and successfully pass the National Council Licensure Examination for Practical Nurses (NCLEX-PN) examination. However, there are exceptions. In California, you can become an LVN by completion of equivalent education and experience: 54 hours of pharmacology, 51 months of paid bedside nursing experience and verification of skill proficiency, or completion of education and experience as a corpsman in the U.S. military—12 months of active duty rendering direct bedside patient care, completion of the basic course in nursing in a branch of the armed forces, and general honorable discharge from the military. Those seeking to become LVNs via these alternatives must still take and pass the NCLEX exam.

LPNs often provide basic bedside care. They gather information from clients, including their health history and present state of health, sometimes using this information to complete medical charts, insurance forms, preauthorizations, and referrals, and they share this information with registered nurses and physicians to help determine the best plan of care for the client. LPNs measure and record clients' height, weight, temperature, blood pressure, pulse, and respiration. They assist clients with bathing, eating, dressing, personal hygiene, and mobility. LPNs collect samples for testing, perform routine laboratory tests, and record food and fluid intake and output. Some LPNs help to deliver, care for, and feed newborns; some care for children; others care for the elderly. In physicians' offices and clinics, LPNs may be responsible for making appointments, keeping records, and performing other clerical duties. Those who work in home healthcare may prepare meals and teach family members how to perform simple nursing tasks. In some states, LPNs are permitted to administer prescribed medicines, start and monitor intravenous (IV) fluids, and provide care to ventilator-dependent patients.

Registered Nurses

With numbers around 2.5 million, registered nurses (RNs) constitute the largest healthcare occupation. Men and women become registered nurses by completing a diploma, associate degree, or baccalaureate degree program and taking the National Council Licensure Examination for Registered Nurses (NCLEX-RN). RNs treat individuals, families, and groups, educate them about various medical conditions, and provide counseling and emotional support. RNs establish or contribute to a plan of care for each client. Care plans may include activities such as administering medication and assessing for effectiveness and reaction; starting, maintaining, and discontinuing intravenous (IV) lines for fluid, medication, blood, and blood products; administering therapies and treatments; observing the patient and recording client care and interactions; and collaborating or consulting with other members of the healthcare team. RNs provide supervision to licensed practical nurses and nursing aides regarding patient care. RNs with advanced educational preparation and training may perform diagnostic and therapeutic procedures and may have prescriptive authority.

RNs can specialize in one or more areas of patient care. They can choose a particular work setting, such as the operating room, emergency center, or even a prison, or they can choose to work with clients who have a specific problem, as do diabetic nurse clinicians or wound care nurses. Some nurses focus on specific body systems, such as cardiac care or head trauma, while still others work with specific populations, including children (pediatric nursing), the elderly (gerontological, or geriatric, nursing) or women's health. Many RNs combine two of these areas, working in specialties such as pediatric oncology (children with cancer) or geropsychiatric nursing (elders with psychiatric problems including Alzheimer's disease). Some RNs may combine specialties. For example, pediatric oncology nurses deal with children and adolescents who have cancer.

Advanced Practice Nurses

Advanced practice nurses (APNs) are registered nurses with additional education, skills, and scope of practice. They deliver high-quality, cost-effective care, particularly to underserved populations, often performing physical examinations, ordering tests, making diagnoses, and prescribing medications. Most APNs possess a master's degree; however, the American Association of Colleges of Nursing (AACN) member institutions voted to change the current level of preparation for advanced nursing practice from the master's degree to the doctorate level by the year 2015.

APN is an umbrella category that includes nurse practitioners, clinical nurse specialists, nurse midwives, and nurse anesthetists:

1. **Nurse practitioners** deliver primary or acute care in clinics, private offices, hospitals, schools, workplaces, and other settings. They perform activities such as conducting physical exams, providing immunizations, diagnosing and treating common illnesses and injuries, and managing common chronic illnesses.
2. **Clinical nurse specialists** provide direct and indirect specialty nurse care to specific patient populations.
3. **Nurse midwives** provide prenatal and gynecological care to healthy women and deliver newborns in hospitals, homes, and birthing centers. They also provide care to the mothers and babies after birth.
4. **Nurse anesthetists** administer more than 65% of anesthetics given to clients each year and are the sole providers of anesthesia in approximately one-third of U.S. hospitals.

Most advanced practice nurses can prescribe medications in all states and the District of Columbia, and many can practice independently without physician collaboration or supervision in several states. Several studies have shown that APNs provide care that is equal to or better than comparable care given by physicians, and they do so at lower cost.

WHO ARE NURSES?

People enter nursing through different career paths. Some enter right after high school, while others become nurses later in life after experiencing other careers. Who are today's nurses? Two U.S. Health Resources and Services Administration (HRSA) surveys provide some answers—the *2004 National Sample Survey of Registered Nurses* and the *2004 Supply, Demand and Use of Practical Nurses.*

Age: The average age of RNs climbed to 46.8, which is the highest average age since the first comparable report published in 1980. About 41% of RNs were 50 years of age or older (41% compared to 25% in 1980), and only 8% were under 30, compared to 25% in 1980. The graying of nursing results from fewer young nurses entering the RN population, large groups of the RNs aging into their 50s and 60s, and older graduates from initial nursing education programs entering the RN population. The average age of LPNs is also increasing. Their mean age in 1984 was 39; in 2001, their mean age was 43.

NURSING NOTES

How I Got into Nursing, by Scott Rosman

My journey into nursing is not exactly what most would consider traditional. Like most little boys growing up, I dreamed of being a firefighter or astronaut and the thought of being a nurse had certainly never crossed my mind.

My senior year of high school I decided to attend BOCES part-time for a computer networking program they offered; I planned to go to college for this the following year. This allowed me to work in the field for the better part of my senior year. Fate works in funny ways sometimes. Through this program I realized that I disliked working with computers and needed to work with people. So when I went to take my placement exams for an associate degree, I met with an academic advisor that same day and requested to change my major to nursing.

I started the nursing program in the fall of 2004, I was 18 years old and one of only a handful of men in the class. I was young and scared and had no idea what I was getting myself into. With the guidance of some amazing people and a whole lot of hard work I made it through nursing school and became a registered nurse. This accomplishment is one of the proudest moments of my life.

Not until I started working as an RN did I truly realize what a great choice I made by going into nursing. Every day is different; every day another life can be touched.

A word of advice for other male nurses, male nursing students, and men considering nursing—don't let the social stigma of men in nursing get to you. It is an antiquated belief that nurses should be women and men in nursing are feminine. Absolutely not the case. Embrace the great work nurses do every day and don't let anyone get under your skin. The need for nurses now is greater than ever, and we cannot afford to lose you *guys*.

Gender: Males still make up a very small percentage of the total RN population at 5.8%, although their numbers are climbing. In the United States, 168,181 of the estimated 2,909,357 RNs are men, but this number represents a 14.5% increase over the 2000 estimate, when 146,902 RNs were male, and a 273.2% increase over 1980, when the population of male RNs was only 45,060. Male RNs are more likely to be younger than their female counterparts, with 30.1% of male RNs under the age of 40 compared to 26.1% of female RNs. Men are a slowly growing share of the LPN workforce, comprising only 3 percent of LPNs in 1984 and 5 percent in 2001, demonstrating a similar growth rate to the RN workforce.

NURSING NOTES

Nursing—Not All That Uniform for Men, by Jerome Scarpati

Becoming a nurse is a tough endeavor and oftentimes some of the most annoying parts of it are the secondary aspects. I remember sophomore year when we were getting ready to start clinical. Our program required us to order our uniforms from a specific online company. As a male nurse, I'll never forget the gist of their slogan,

something like: "Nursing Uniforms: made for women by women." Needless to say the
pants never fit right.

Race/Ethnicity: In 2004, the number of nurses identifying their racial/ethnic background as one or more nonwhite groups, Hispanic, or Latino numbered 311,177 (10.7%), representing a decrease of 22,190 from 2000, but nearly triple the number of nonwhite, Hispanic, or Latino nurses in 1980. However, HRSA noted that the decline may have resulted from an increase in the number of RNs who did not completely specify their combined racial or ethnic background. The number of non-Hispanic Asian or Other Pacific Islander RNs showed the highest relative increase at 167.8% from 33,600 in 1980 to 89,977 in 2004. The number of nurses from Hispanic or Latino backgrounds increased by 203.8%, from 20,816 in 1980 to 63,240 in 2004, while the number of RNs reporting American Indian or Alaska Native non-Hispanic backgrounds increased by 122.5% from 4,249 in 1980 to 9,453 in 2004. The increase for Black or African American non-Hispanic RNs over the same period is an estimated 101.3%, rising from 60,845 in 1980 to 122,495 in 2004. The LPN population is predominantly white, although ethnic diversity has grown. In 1984, 77% of LPNs were white, but this share dropped to 67% by 2001. Blacks or African Americans make up the largest minority group of LPNs, comprising 26% of the workforce in 2001. Hispanics account for 3%, Asians account for 2%, and Native Americans account for 1% of the LPN workforce.

Family status: In the 2004 survey, the majority (70.5%) of RNs were married, 18.1% were separated, divorced or widowed, and 9.2% had never married. About 42.5% of RNs had children under 18 living in their household. Almost 16% were caring for other adults in their home, while 15.5% were caring for other adults living elsewhere. The majority of RNs (52.1%) have both children and other adults at home. Most LPNs were married (56% to 66%). Between 23% and 32% were separated, divorced, or widowed, and 10% to 14% had never married.

The HRSA LPN survey also used data from the Bureau of Labor Statistics Current Population Survey to compare and contrast LPNs and RNs, summing up with the following:

Similarities

▶ Both the LPN and RN populations are aging.

▶ Males represent a small but increasing percentage of both populations.

▶ The western United States has the lowest numbers of LPNs and RNs relative to the population.

▶ LPNs and RNs work an average of 36 to 38 hours per week.

▶ The percentage of LPNs and RNs working in physician offices and clinics doubled between 1984 and 2001.

▶ The hourly pay rate of LPNs and RNs increased 19% between 1984 and 2001.

Differences

▶ The LPN population is smaller than the RN population, but the actual size of the LPN workforce is unclear because the available data are conflicting.

▶ Compared to RNs, fewer LPNs live in the Northeast and more live in the South.

▶ An increasing percentage of RNs are immigrants, while fewer LPNs are foreign-born.

▶ More RNs than LPNs work in hospitals.

▶ The percentage of LPNs working in nursing and personal care facilities increased between 1984 and 2001. The RN percentage did not.

▶ As of 2001, the percentage of LPNs working in the private sector was greater than the percentage of RNs working in the private sector.

THE NURSING PROCESS

Regardless of practice area or specialty, nurses use the same framework of nursing care, called the nursing process. The American Nurses Association describes the nursing process as the crucial core of practice delivering holistic, client-focused nursing care. Originally a five-phase process, the nursing process today consists of six phases: assessment, diagnosis, outcomes identification, planning, implementation, and evaluation.

Assessment: Assessment is the systematic collection of subjective (what the client says) and objective (what the nurse sees, hears, smells, and feels) information from the client. During this phase, nurses consider the physical, psychological, sociocultural, and spiritual factors that may affect the client's health situation. Nurses perform initial, comprehensive assessments when they first admit a client to a hospital setting, when they accept a new client into a physician's office or clinic, and when they first visit a home healthcare client. These assessments are quite detailed and require significant time to perform because of the amount of data needed when clients have problems that have yet to be identified. Nurses complete focused assessments on clients whose problem has been identified to note whether that problem has worsened, improved, or resolved. These assessments are shorter in duration and more concise, and they are typically performed on a regular basis. For example, a nurse working in an intensive care unit may assess a client's blood pressure every few minutes. Time-elapsed visits also require nursing assessment. These vary in duration and frequency, depending on the client's health issues. Examples include annual health visits for children or interval assessments for weight reduction. The last but crucial type is emergency assessment for life-threatening situations when nurses must remember their ABCs—airway, breathing, and circulation, especially for clients with heart or lung problems. Nurses must also have emergency psychological skills in order to assess clients who may want to kill themselves or harm others.

Diagnosis: While APNs can make medical diagnoses, most nurses cannot. Nurses diagnose human responses to actual or potential health problems after analyzing and interpreting the data they collect from their assessment. The North American Nursing Diagnosis Association (NANDA) defines nursing diagnosis as "a clinical judgment about individual, family or community responses to actual or potential health problems or life processes, which provide the basis for selection of nursing interventions to achieve outcomes for which the nurse is accountable." Nursing diagnoses guide the selection of interventions that are likely to produce the desired treatment effects and determine nurse-sensitive outcomes. They also provide a means of communicating client care requirements to other nurses.

Outcomes identification: Nurses use assessments and diagnoses to create measurable and achievable short- and long-term goals. The newest addition to the nursing process, outcome identification, provides individualized care, promotes client participation, plans care that is realistic and measurable, and allows for the involvement of support personnel. Nurses use their knowledge and skills to prioritize client outcomes. High priorities include life-threatening situations like hemorrhaging, events that require immediate attention such as discharge planning, and issues that are extremely important to the client such as pain. Low priorities involve problems that usually resolve with little attention, such as discomfort from minor surgery.

Planning: Planning refers to the development of nursing strategies that can alleviate the client's problems. To meet the standards of the Joint Commission for Accreditation of Healthcare Organizations (JCAHO), the plan must be developed by an RN, documented in the client's healthcare record, and reflect the standards of care established by the institution and the profession. Medicare and Medicaid, and some third-party reimbursement plans (e.g., health insurance) require care plans for each client.

Implementation: Nurses implement client care according to the care plan to assure the continuity of care during hospitalization, discharge, and home care. The purpose of this action phase of the nursing process is to provide individualized therapeutic and technical care to help the client achieve an optimal level of health. Nurses may delegate some interventions to other members of the healthcare team; however, RNs maintain the responsibility and accountability for the supervision and evaluation of these personnel.

Evaluation: RNs continuously evaluate both the client's status and the effectiveness of the client's care. They then modify the care plan as needed. During this phase, nurses conduct a thorough, systematic review of the effectiveness of their nursing interventions and a determination of client goal achievement. The nurse appraises goal attainment jointly with the client. While evaluation is a distinct phase, it occurs throughout the nursing process to assure prompt reassessment, rediagnosing, and replanning when needed.

NURSING NOTES

Making a Difference, One Patient at a Time, by Jolynn Sannicandro

My preceptor and I stood outside a room as she gave me the report on a patient who was admitted that morning. She explained to me that the patient was fresh out of surgery for a total laryngectomy and that the patient's voice box had been completely removed due to laryngeal cancer. My preceptor further identified my objectives for the morning, which included assessing the patient from head to toe, obtaining vital signs every four hours, monitoring output, suctioning the patient, changing the patient's feeding tubes, and providing wound care.

As my preceptor left to tend to another patient, I took a deep breath and walked into the patient's room. She was sitting in a chair with her feet elevated on a stool and a trachea collar attached to oxygen and humidified air. There were two drains located below the right and left clavicles, which appeared to be patent based on the accumulation of fluid. I grasped the stethoscope around my neck and proceeded to introduce myself. As I began my full body assessment, I observed other devices attached to the patient that I had learned about in lecture and seen in clinical practice, such as a catheter and a nasogastric tube. The catheter was properly placed by the nurse. It was taut against her thigh and below the bladder. The nasogastric tube was connected to a pump and there was formula flowing from the feeding bag through the tube and into the patient. The woman had a nervous but kind smile and warm eyes behind thick round glasses. The patient's fear for her own well-being was compounded by her awareness of my own self-doubt. This being only my second day at this hospital, I was still experiencing the butterflies that come with every unfamiliar and challenging experience. However, I placed my own apprehension aside and thought back to the nursing classes that had more than adequately prepared me for the current situation I was in, dealing with a patient who was scared and needed a medical professional who she could trust. I had no idea that this initial placing of trust would be the beginning of the kind of relationship that is at the heart of the nursing profession.

The patient remained under the hospital's care for several weeks. I was assigned this same patient every clinical rotation and began to grow closer to her. Although communicating was difficult because everything she wanted to say to me had to be written on a notepad, I was still able to read her emotionally by looking for nonverbal cues. As a nursing student I had been trained to become more aware of a patient's emotional state by observing for something as subtle as a slight change in a patient's facial expression.

I was also able to glimpse the life of the patient through her large, close-knit family, who visited her daily. I came to know the patient's family when they would visit her to play board games, watch her favorite soap opera, or share stories about their day. Throughout these visits I saw the interactions the family members had with the patient and quickly realized how important her family was to her.

One day after a visit by the family members I was checking the patient's vital signs; she tapped me on the shoulder to show me a note she had just written on her pad that said, "Do you think I will be out of here in a month to see my niece get married?" Taking her hand in mine I told her that I could not promise her when she would be discharged from the hospital, because I did not want to instill in her a false sense of hope. However, I assured her that the healthcare professionals and I would be there with her every step of the way on her journey toward recovery. With that, the patient gave me a smile and squeezed my hand.

After I assured the patient that I would be there for her, I made sure she continued to build her strength by walking around the floor with her, washing her hair, or just simply spending time with her when her family was not there. As I did these things, I could see before my own eyes that her health and morale were slowly improving. This pattern continued for several weeks before she was finally discharged from the hospital. On her last day, the day before her niece's wedding, she wrote me one last note that said, " I couldn't have done this without you; I love you." After giving her a hug and a kiss, I realized that moments like this are why I wake up early for clinical and spend long hours in the library. I truly felt, and her note confirmed, that I was an integral part of this woman's recovery. The experience I encountered with this patient showed me that this career allows me to touch the lives of people in ways that people in other fields will never get to experience.

STANDARDS OF NURSING PRACTICE

The American Nurses Association (ANA) developed general and specialty-specific standards of nursing practice that provide guidelines for nursing practice. These standards are the rules of competent care, and RNs are required by law to carry out care in accordance with what other reasonably prudent nurses would do in the same or similar situations. The American Nurses Association standards consist of three components: (1) professional standards of care define diagnostic, intervention, and evaluation competencies; (2) professional standards identify role functions in direct care, consultation, and quality assurance; and (3) specialty practice guidelines are protocols for specific client populations. The ANA standards are comprised of standards of care and standards of professional practice. The standards of care are based on the nursing process and describe a competent level of nursing care. Standards of professional performance cover quality of care, performance appraisal, education, collegiality, ethics, collaboration, research, and resource utilization.

American Nurses Association standards of care for specialty-specific nursing practice include, but are not limited to: addictions nursing practice, cardiovascular nursing, corrections nursing, faith community nursing, genetics/genomic nursing, gerontological nursing, HIV/AIDS nursing, holistic nursing, home health nursing, hospice and palliative nursing, intellectual and developmental disabilities nursing, legal nurse consulting nursing, neonatal nursing, neuroscience nursing, nursing administration, nursing informatics, nursing professional development, pain management nursing, pediatric nursing, plastic surgery nursing, psychiatric nursing, public health nursing, radiology nursing, school nursing, and vascular nursing. The scope and standards of practice for forensic nursing is due out in 2009.

The ANA, along with its 54 constituent organizations, is the only full-service professional organization representing the nation's 2.9 million registered nurses, but it is not the only nursing organization, nor is it the only one to have standards of care and scope of practice for nurses. Several specialty nursing organizations also provide these guidelines for those nurses within their specialties. The National Association of Pediatric Nurse Practitioners and Associates (NAPNAP) and the Society of Pediatric Nurses (SPN) created unified standards and scope of practice for pediatric nurses; the American College of Nurse Midwives developed standards of care for nurse midwives; and the American Association of Nurse Anesthetists developed the scope and standards of care for nurse anesthetists. JCAHO, an organization that accredits healthcare facilities, sets standards for aspects of nursing care, such as documentation.

Nurses are also held accountable for employer standards of practice, which are frequently written as policies and procedures. For example, hospitals that allow nurses to start intravenous therapy will most likely have standards of practice for that intervention.

STATE BOARDS OF NURSING AND NURSE PRACTICE ACTS

All 50 states, the District of Columbia, and U.S. territories Guam, the Virgin Islands, American Samoa, and the Mariana Islands have boards that oversee nurses in their jurisdictions. Boards are appointed by the governor and usually consist of RNs, LPNs, and consumers. State boards may be independent agencies of the state government or part of a department or bureau, such as the department of licensure and regulation. Most boards govern practical, registered, and advanced practice nurses, while others have separate boards for practical nurses. As examples, the Kentucky Board of Nursing governs all nurses; the California Board of Registered Nursing oversees registered and advanced practice nurses, while the California Bureau of Vocation Nursing and Psychiatric Technicians oversees practical nurses. All boards are members of the National Council of State Boards of Nursing (NCSBN), which provides leadership to advance regulatory excellence for public protection.

Nursing boards regulate the practice of practical, registered, and advanced practice nurses in order to promote nursing quality and to protect the health and safety of the public. State boards of nursing are authorized to develop responsibilities, regulations, and rules related to the state nursing practice act and to enforce the rules to obtain and maintain licensure. They also approve nursing education programs, provide nurse practice acts, and handle complaints against nurses.

Boards of nursing are authorized to approve all new nursing education programs within their state. Educational institutions proposing the development of a new nursing education program are required to submit a feasibility study addressing their intent. Typically, the Board provides provisional or initial approval after making a site visit, and then full approval after the program receives the NCLEX results on the majority of the first graduating class that provide evidence that the program meets all state requirements. State board approval is important for nursing programs because it demonstrates that the program meets the state's standards for nursing education. But it is even more important for you because you cannot take the NCLEX exam, and thus be licensed to practice nursing, unless you graduate from a state board-approved nursing program.

State boards of nursing and state nurses associations usually collaborate in the initiation and revision of the state nurse practice act that defines nursing practice in their jurisdiction. These practice acts are state laws that govern nursing practice and, in some areas, nursing education and protecting the safety and welfare of the public. Nurse practice acts usually define the board of nursing's composition, authority, and power; define nursing, as well as its boundaries and scope of practice; identify and protect types of titles; identify types of licenses and their requirements; and identify the grounds for disciplinary action.

Learning About Your State Practice Act

To learn about your area's Nurse Practice Act, contact your state board of nursing, as found in Appendix A.

Consumers and professionals can file a complaint with the state board of nursing when they believe that a nurse has acted in a manner that is illegal or irresponsible in regard to professional nursing practice. The boards and/or another state-delegated agency review all complaints and investigate those who warrant an inquiry. The board may determine that a case does not require action based on board disciplinary policies, or it may determine that no rule or law violations occurred. They may also decide that a complaint requires disciplinary action that may include:

▶ a fine—a specific amount of money that must be paid to the state
▶ a reprimand—a formal notice stating that standards have been violated
▶ probation—a period of time during which the nurse must practice under specified restrictions or conditions that may affect the nurse's job role and setting
▶ suspension—a period of time during which the nurse's license is suspended and during which the nurse may not practice nursing
▶ revocation—removal of a nursing license for an unspecified time; may be permanent
▶ voluntary surrender—nurse is asked to give up license rather than face suspension or revocation
▶ denial of licensure—the board will not issue a license

Typically, complaint reviews and investigations are kept confidential, but disciplinary action is made public and may be posted on the state board of nursing's Internet site.

NURSING ETHICS

Ethics deals with standards of conduct and moral judgment. The major principles of healthcare ethics that must be upheld in all situations are beneficence, nonmaleficence, autonomy, and justice. *Beneficence* means promoting or doing good. Nurses work to promote their clients' best interests and strive to achieve optimal outcomes. *Nonmaleficence* means avoiding harm. Nurses must maintain a competent practice level to avoid causing injury or suffering to clients. The principle of nonmaleficence also covers reporting suspected abuse to prevent further victimization and protecting clients from chemically impaired nurses and other healthcare practitioners. Autonomy stands for independence and the ability to be self-directed. Clients have the right of self-determination and are entitled to decide what happens to them; therefore, competent adults have the capacity to consent to or refuse treatment. Nurses must respect the client's wishes, even if they don't agree with them. Finally, justice requires that all clients be treated equally and fairly. Nurses face issues of justice daily when organizing care for their clients and deciding how much time they will spend with each based on client needs and a fair distribution of resources.

Nurses need to distinguish between their personal values and their professional ethics. Personal values are what nurses hold significant and true for themselves, while professional ethics involve principles that have universal applications and standards of conduct that must be upheld in all situations. Nurses thus avoid allowing personal judgments to bias client care. They are honest and fair with clients, and they act in the best interest of and show respect for them.

Since nurses address complex ethical and human rights issues on a regular basis, the American Nurses Association Board of Directors and the Congress on Nursing Practice first initiated the *Code of Ethics for Nurses* in 1985 to delineate the code of responsibilities and conduct expected of nurses in their practice. Nurses are held responsible to comply with the standards of ethical practice and to ensure that other nurses also comply. The code was revised in 2001 to include issues of advancing nursing science and is based on the opinions and experience of a wide range of nurses. The ANA approved nine provisions that address ethical practice issues such as compassion and respect, the nurse's primary commitment to the patient, patient advocacy, responsibility and accountability, duties, participation in the healthcare environment, advancement of the profession, and collaboration. You can read or purchase the ANA *Code of Ethics for Nurses with Interpretive Statements* at www.nursingworld.org.

LEGAL ISSUES IN NURSING

A number of legal issues are related to nursing practice, including licensing, nurse practice acts, and standards of care. However, in these litigious times, the issue that most concerns those considering a career in nursing are negligence and malpractice. Negligence is either an act of omission (not doing something a reasonably prudent person would do) or commission (doing something a reasonably prudent person would not do). Malpractice is negligence by a professional. Four elements are needed to prove malpractice:

1. **Duty:** Duty stands for a legal obligation owed by one person to another person. When nurses care for clients, they assume the duty to care for them in a competent and diligent manner. Nurses are expected to provide the degree of care ordinarily exercised by other nurses practicing in the same nursing specialty. Therefore, nurses are expected to adhere to standards of care—those imposed by the nurse's state board of nursing nurse practice act, the national nursing specialty standards of care and scope of practice, and the nurse's hospital, or other agency, protocols.

2. **Breach:** A breach of duty takes place when there is failure to fulfill the duties established as being the responsibility of the nurse. In other words, nurses breach their duty when they do not meet the appropriate standard of care.

3. **Causation:** Causation is the most difficult element to prove because it is the factual connection between what the nurse did and the injury to the client. Causation means that the nurse's breach of duty, or failure to meet the appropriate standard of care, caused the client's injury or adverse outcome.

4. **Damages:** Damages are monetary payments designed to compensate the client for the injury or adverse outcome, and are intended to restore

the plaintiff to the condition he or she was in prior to the injury. To re-cover damages, the client must establish that he or she suffered physi-cal, financial, or emotional injury caused by the nurse's violation of the standard of care. Damages are usually compensatory or punitive.

Nurses and nursing students can be held liable for their actions, and thus can be sued. However, the majority of nurses are competent professionals who provide a satisfactory level of care. According to HRSA's 2003 National Practitioner Data Bank (NPDB), only about 1 in 50 malpractice payment reports were for nurses. All levels of RNs were responsible for 4,512, or 1.8%, of malpractice payments over the history of the NPDB. Other classi-fied RNs were responsible for 63.3%, and included nurse anesthetists, nurse midwives, and nurse practitioners. Reasons for malpractice payment reports varied depending on the type of nurse, but included monitoring, treatment, and medication problems.

High-level-need clients and short staffing can increase the chances for error, but nurses can minimize their liability by focusing on risk management. Healthcare facilities provide various levels of in-service education on risk man-agement, and nurses can take continuing education courses on this important topic. Some states require risk management education courses for license initi-ation and/or renewal. Florida requires a course on reducing medical errors, while Ohio requires nurses to take a course to become familiar with their state nurse practice act. Taking a risk management course can also have some mon-etary advantage—some nursing malpractice insurance companies give dis-counts on premiums to those who complete a risk management course.

NURSING AND THE PATIENT CARE PARTNERSHIP

Ethical client care requires that nurses respect client rights. The American Hospital Association (AHA) first adopted the Patient Bill of Rights in 1973. The purpose was to contribute to more effective patient care with rights that were supported by the hospital on behalf of the institution, its medical staff, employees, and patients. The bill was replaced in 2003 by the Patient Care Partnership that informs patients about what they should expect dur-ing their hospital stay with regard to both their rights and responsibilities.

The goal of the Patient Care Partnership is for clients and their families to have the same attention and care that healthcare providers would want for themselves and their families: high quality care; a clean and safe environment; involvement in their care; protection of their privacy; help when leaving the hospital; and help with their billing. These rights are available for clients to read in several languages.

NURSING AND THE CHANGING HEALTHCARE ENVIRONMENT

The healthcare system has a dramatic impact on nursing practice, and nursing practice has a dramatic impact on the healthcare system. At the beginning of the 1900s nurses made home visits and tended to the needs of the sick. Hospitals soon became the hub of healthcare delivery, and nurses provided nursing care. Nursing education evolved, and the practice of nursing expanded. In the 1970s and 1980s nurses sought more autonomy, especially with regard to hospital administration and physicians—one of the reasons for the development and increase of nurse practitioners. At this same time, healthcare costs began to drastically rise, creating a congressional demand for cost containment related to Medicare—government health insurance for people 65 and older, people under 65 with certain disabilities, and people of any age with permanent kidney failure. This demand began with prospective payment through diagnosis-related groups (DRGs), and health insurance companies joined in the demand, forcing hospital administrators to cut costs to survive.

While hospitals remain a crucial component of the healthcare system, they are but part of the maze. Rising costs have moved more procedures, treatments, and surgeries into ambulatory (outpatient) settings. People seeking healthcare today face a variety of settings for services that revolve around health promotion, illness prevention, diagnostic testing, treatment, surgical procedures, rehabilitation, and supportive and palliative care. All these settings need nurses, opening new avenues for career paths since a nursing license allows nurses to work in numerous settings without the need of additional education.

Healthcare changes, coupled with a troubled economy, have left a growing number of people with no health insurance. According to the National

Coalition on Health Care, almost 46 million Americans (18% of the population under 65) had no health insurance in 2007. Lack of insurance means decreased access to health care for many Americans, but nursing has stepped in to assist with this crisis. Nurses throughout the United States bridge the healthcare gaps to the indigent and uninsured through nurse-run clinics, university- and hospital-based programs, public health services, and community programs such as parish nursing. These nursing roles provide much needed care to an often forgotten population, and they provide nurses with opportunities for more autonomous practice.

Medical advances and technology affect nursing practice. Medical advances have resulted in an explosion of diagnostic and monitoring equipment, as well as new pharmacological preparations and surgical procedures. Some of these advances have made nurses' lives easier, while others have increased their responsibilities and educational needs. Digital thermometers save time, but the proliferation of new and potent drugs creates constant need to update knowledge on these drugs' expected actions, adverse effects, and compatibility with other drugs. Many of today's medical advances have resulted in new job venues, giving nurses the opportunity to work in diagnostic centers and ambulatory surgery centers.

Technology now gives us computerized record keeping and resources. Clipboards have been replaced by laptops, textbooks by PDAs (personal digital assistants). Telehealth uses technology to provide healthcare over distance by allowing physicians to diagnose and treat patients via the Internet. Telehealth technologies reduce cost, improve access to care, facilitate client-provider communications, and remove the barriers of time and distance. It is especially beneficial in rural areas where healthcare access is limited by provider shortages, lack of insurance, and geographical distance to healthcare facilities. These and other technological advances have resulted in the specialty of nursing informatics and the inclusion of healthcare technology into basic nursing education.

Nursing informatics isn't the only specialty to come out of healthcare changes in the past few decades. Others include hospice nursing, forensic nursing, legal nurse consulting, transplant nursing, holistic nursing, HIV/AIDS nursing, international nursing, toxicology nursing, and the nursing entrepreneur. This list is incomplete and still growing, and these and other nursing specialties are discussed in Chapter 6.

THE NURSING SHORTAGE

The nursing shortage is of such huge consequence that it merits more than mere mention. The United States is entrenched in a nursing shortage that will only intensify as baby boomers age and healthcare needs grow. In 2007, the U.S. Bureau of Labor Statistics projected the need for one million new and replacement nurses by 2016, with an estimated 587,000 new nursing positions created through 2016, making nursing the nation's top profession in terms of projected job growth. The U.S. Health Resources and Services Administration (HRSA) estimates that the nation's nursing shortage will grow to more than one million nurses by the year 2020.

According to a research report, titled *The Future of the Nursing Workforce in the United States: Data, Trends and Implications* and written by Peter Buerhaus, PhD, of Vanderbilt University School of Nursing, Douglas Staiger, PhD, from Dartmouth University, and David Auerbach, PhD, of the Congressional Budget Office, the demand for RNs is expected to grow at 2% to 3% per year, as it has done for the past four decades, while the supply of RNs is expected to grow very little as large numbers of nurses begin to retire. These researchers further noted that the current shortage began in 1998, making it the longest lasting nursing shortage in the past 50 years. The inadequate number of nurses in hospitals has disastrous consequences, as it is associated with reductions in patient capacity, delays in the timeliness of patient care, longer length of hospital stays by patients, interruptions in the healthcare delivery processes, and increased risk of adverse patient outcomes including death.

The American Association of Colleges of Nursing (AACN) and the U.S. Health Resources and Services Administration (HRSA) list several factors that led to the shortage. The first is that enrollment in nursing programs has not grown fast enough to meet the demands. HRSA notes that the United States must graduate approximately 90% more nurses from its nursing programs to meet the estimated growth in demand for RN services. Reasons for the lackluster growth include the increased opportunity for women in the workforce today and a decline in public perception of the attractiveness of nursing as a profession. A second factor is workforce participation. The active supply of RNs is defined as the number of licensed RNs who provide nursing care or who are actively seeking employment in nursing. This supply excludes licensed RNs who are retired, who have temporarily left nursing, and who are working in non-nursing positions. The shortage creates more shortage because some nurses leave their jobs because of the stress from insufficient staffing.

Changing demographics present a third factor. An influx of aging baby boomers will create significant demands on the healthcare system with their needs for wellness opportunities, technological advances, and long-term care—all of which will require more nurses to meet these needs. This increase in older adults will be considerable. According to the National Center for Policy Analysis (NCPA), in 2000 about 35 million people, or 13% of the U.S. population, were 65 and older, but by 2030 that number will rise to 70 million, or 20% of the population. The growth rate for those 85 and older will be an estimated 56%, and this population is even more likely to have healthcare problems that warrant nursing care.

Baby boomers also make up a considerable portion of the nursing population. HRSA's 2005 National Sample Survey of Registered Nurses noted that the average age of RNs was estimated at 46.8 years of age, more than four years older than in 1996 when the average age was 42.3, and a report by the U.S. Government Accounting Office predicts that 40% of RNs will be older than 50 by 2010. In one of his other studies, Buerhaus noted that the current RN workforce will retire in large numbers over the next decade, just as those 80 million baby boomers reach 65 and consume more healthcare.

But baby boomers aren't the only ones guzzling up healthcare. Hospital clients are sicker today than they were 20 years ago. This increase in acuity means that nurses should care for fewer patients than they did in the past because each patient requires more nursing care.

Finally, there is also a nursing faculty shortage, resulting in programs needing to limit their number of students. This shortage, too, is all about supply and demand. One survey showed that 33,000 qualified applicants to nursing programs were turned down and that 76.1% of the surveyed schools indicated that the faculty shortage was the main reason for limiting admissions. Meeting the demand for new nurses by 2020 will also require a significant increase in the demand for nursing faculty. And if hospitals seek nurses with BSNs, the demand for faculty may further increase because the ratio of faculty to students in BSN programs is higher than for other forms of entry level programs.

While most of the nursing shortage literature focuses on RNs, LPNs also play a role. The number of LPNs working in hospitals has plummeted by 153,000, or 47%, in the past 20 years. The decrease primarily resulted from the cuts in nursing staff in the 1990s and the shift from team nursing to primary nursing as the prevailing practice model. But some states show an overall decrease in their number of LPNs. A Pennsylvania Center for Health Careers report shows that the LPN shortage in Pennsylvania will likely be as large as 4,100 by 2010. North Dakota reported a shortage of 200 in 2003 with the predicted decrease in LPN numbers.

Now for the good news. State legislatures and boards of nursing have been addressing the problem. Researchers at Vanderbilt University's Center for Interdisciplinary Health Workforce Studies found that the nursing shortage is lessening. The number of nurses has steadily increased since 2006. Dr. Buerhaus reported that 84,200 nursed entered practice in 2007. He now predicts a shortage of 285,000 nurses by 2020, a number considerably lower than previous projections. Dr. Buerhaus still sees the lack of nurses as a threat to the healthcare system and a sign that there is a need for well-trained, qualified nurses.

What does all this shortage doom and gloom mean for you? It means opportunity. You certainly need to consider the stressors related to working during a nursing shortage, but more importantly, you should consider the advantages. The shortage has helped to increase nursing salaries and improve benefits. Many hospitals offer incentive programs such as recruitment bonuses (ranging anywhere from $2,000 to $20,000), relocation assistance, housing assistance, day care, and tuition reimbursement. You are better able to pick and choose the job you want, and you have greater flexibility for mobility since openings abound. Hospitals may have sicker clients, but other clients are in other settings, offering more variety for your career.

Things are also improving partially due to the increase in second-degree students entering the nursing profession. While many of these students entered the nursing profession after September 11, 2001, to "make a difference," this increase also means that there are people out there who are either dissatisfied with other professions or in need of a job. The *Pittsburgh Tribune-Review* ran an article in 2007 titled "Nursing hot choice for second career in PA," and mentioned a man who entered nursing after being laid off as an electrical engineer. One study showed that second-degree students choose nursing because of the salary and employment opportunities, the flexibility of their work schedule, and the positive experience they had with nurses who cared for family members.

These are but a few advantages and disadvantages to weigh when considering a nursing career. Chapter 2 explores these and more in greater detail.

CHAPTER two

THE PROS AND CONS OF NURSING

ONE NURSE'S pro is another's con. If you love to interact with people, you can choose psychiatric nursing; if not, you may prefer perioperative nursing. Nursing is such a versatile profession that there's something in it for almost everyone. But nursing isn't for everyone. It can often be as challenging as it is rewarding. Weigh the good with the bad to see if nursing sounds like the career for you.

THE PROS

Nurses are in demand, and there are abundant job opportunities, good salaries, and decent benefits to prove it. Nursing also allows for flexible scheduling, interesting specialties, and a variety of job settings, topped off with plenty of room for advancement. But the biggest advantage to being a nurse is the satisfaction that comes from knowing you make a difference in people's lives.

Nurses Are in Demand

It's a fact of life. Almost everyone gets sick at some point in their life, making nursing a recession-resistant profession. And nurses are in short supply. A January 6, 2009 Associated Press article noted that the nursing industry is frantic for hires. One company lavished registered nurses with free champagne and a trivia contest hosted by game show veteran Chuck Woolery. Prizes included a one-year lease for a 2009 SUV, a hotel stay, and dinners.

Post-secondary education is an investment, regardless whether you complete a one-year program at a vocational school or a four-year degree at an Ivy League university. Nursing makes that investment pay off. It is not unusual for nursing students to have jobs waiting for them when they graduate. Lamar University boasts 100% employment within six months for their nursing students, and 98% of their senior nursing students have job offers before graduation.

Numerous Job Opportunities

The Bureau of Labor Statistics predicts that the need for RN employment will grow considerably faster than the average for all occupations through 2016, resulting in many new jobs. Registered nurses should generate 587,000 new jobs, among the largest number of new jobs for any occupation. Additionally, hundreds of thousands of job openings will appear as experienced nurses leave the occupation. The job growth rate is predicted to be highest in private and public hospitals, physician offices, home healthcare, outpatient centers, mental health centers, employment services, and nursing care facilities.

The Bureau of Labor Statistics projects the same employment boom for practical nurses, with a 14% growth between now and 2016. Job prospects are expected to be very good, depending on the industry, because, like RN positions, applicants will be needed to replace those LPNs who are leaving the occupation. Most LPN opportunities will be in nursing care facilities due to the numbers of older persons and people with disabilities and in home health agencies because of the increasing number of aging people with functional disabilities who prefer to be treated at home and who can because of new technology.

On one day in early 2009, Medhunters.com listed 4,023 nursing jobs in 17 different nursing areas. Acute care nurses topped the list with 967 openings, followed by advanced practice nurses (786 openings), critical care nurses (456 openings), and nursing management (474 openings). Numbers and types of jobs vary by location, but you still can find jobs, be they urban, suburban, or rural.

Opportunities for Career Advancement

Advancement opportunities abound. LPNs can become charge nurses, particularly in long-term care facilities. However, most advancement opportunities exist for RNs. You can climb the administration ladder and become a nurse manager or supervisor, often without additional education. You can also pursue a graduate degree to move to the top of the heap and become a director of nursing or you can choose to become an advanced practice nurse. Advanced practice nursing requires a master's degree at this point, but the American Association of Colleges of Nursing raised the bar, and the doctor of nursing practice will be the required degree in 2015. You can also choose to become a nurse educator, which also requires additional education if you wish this to be your full-time career.

But advancement does not always mean moving up; you can also make lateral moves. Your nursing license allows you to move among nursing specialties. Six months to a year of acute care experience is often enough to get a job in critical care or emergency nursing. You can also literally move. Nurses who work with nurse-for-hire agencies can hospital shop and work at various locations, often making good money and getting to work the hours of their choosing. If that's not enough movement, you can become a travel nurse, which allows you to work at your own pace and make your own decisions. Travel nursing also allows you to work in your own hometown or hundreds of miles away.

Travel nursing was listed as one of the Top Five Hot Careers in Nursing by AllNursingSchools.com in January 2009. The other four were military nursing, forensic nursing, legal nurse consulting, and surgical nursing. As the demand for nurses rises, so does the realization of how nurses fit into less typical settings.

Salaries

The Bureau of Labor Statistics showed the median annual earnings of LPNs at $36,550 in May 2006, with the middle 50% of LPNs earning between $31,080 and $43, 640. The highest 10% earned more than $50,480, while the lowest 10% earned $26,380. Median salaries per job location in May 2006 were:

employment services	$42,110
nurse care facilities	$38,320
home healthcare agencies	$37,880
hospitals	$35,000
physician offices	$32,710

The Advance for LPNs 2008 LPN Salary Survey broke down salaries by state. Alaskan LPNs made top dollar at $29 per hour, but the survey creators advised that there were only four respondents from Alaska. LPNs in the Northeast fared best, with Connecticut LPNs earning as much as $25.28 per hour. States with the lowest hour rates included Alabama ($16.93), Nebraska ($15.75), North Dakota ($15.00), and Idaho ($14.67).

The U.S. Census Bureau's 2006 National Survey shows that RNs can earn about $15,000 more per year than LPNs. According to Allnursing schools.com, LPNs with 15 years until retirement can earn an additional

$25,000 if they simply invest another 12 months in completing an online LPN-to-RN program.

For RNs, the Bureau of Labor Statistics reports median annual earnings of $57,280 in May 2006. The middle 50% of RNs earned between $47,710 and $69,850, while the top 10% earned more than $83,440, and the bottom 10%, less than $40, 250. Median RN salaries per job location in May 2006 were:

employment services	$64,260
nursc case facilities	$58,550
home healthcare agencies	$54,190
hospitals	$53,800
physician offices	$52,490

The Advance Salary Survey 2008 listed the average RN nursing salary at $56,785. Not all states participated, but of those that did, California had the highest state average at $71,474, followed by New York ($63,132) and Delaware ($61,679). The states with the lowest salaries were Alabama ($47,688), Maine ($46,127), and Tennessee ($43,820).

Advanced degrees mean higher salaries that vary per practice type. Advance for Nurse Practitioners 2007 National Salary Survey showed that the average NP salary was $81,397. Pay Scale Inc. had average salaries for nurse midwives and nurse anesthetists. Nurse midwives who were in practice for less than a year earned an average $57,767 and those who practiced 10 to 19 years earned $48,000 (yes, the more experienced ones earned less). Nurse anesthetists earn the most with those practicing less than one year earning an average of $113,728 and those in practice for 20 years or more earning $141,578.

Benefits

Most hospitals and other agencies offer sick leave, paid holidays, vacation time, shift differential, occupational health services, employee assistance programs, health insurance benefits, and retirement plans. Others also offer additional benefits or discounted services that include: short- and long-term disability plans, life insurance, long-term care insurance, tax-sheltered annuities, credit unions, and parking.

The nursing shortage has given rise to a wide range of benefits as an incentive to fill their mounting vacancies. Some of these include:

► Sign-on bonuses that can range from $500 to $20,000. These typically require that you stay employed at that facility for a period of time—the longer the time, the bigger the bonus.
► Tuition reimbursement. You can advance your education at little to no cost.
► Relocation assistance. This makes it easier for you to uproot your family to a new location.
► Housing assistance. Employment facility-owned housing can also cost less per month.
► Day care. Day care on the worksite or nearby decreases your out-of-pocket expenses for child care.

Flexible Scheduling

The need for nurses has increased the availability of flexible schedules for both full- and part-time employees. Hospitals and other agencies often offer 4-, 8-, 10-, and 12-hour shifts and allow you to work weekdays, weekends, or both. Twelve-hour shifts sound, and often are, grueling. But working three 12-hour days per week usually means you are off for the other four days. Flexible shifts are especially helpful for working parents, allowing one of them to be available to the children at all times.

Opportunities for Self-Employment

Many nurses have struck out on their own, combining their nursing knowledge with business know-how. Some have their own businesses and even employ other nurses, while others are independent contractors. Practicing independently gives you more autonomy, more income, and more control over your professional life.

Making a Difference

You can help bring a baby into the world, hold a lonely elder's hand when she dies, breathe life back into a man who had a heart attack, lift a depressed person's spirits, or ease the pain of an injured child. Few careers give you the opportunity to impact on so many lives in so many different ways. There is no greater benefit than having a client thank you for making them feel better. As a nurse you can, and will, make a difference.

THE CONS

No job is perfect, and nursing is no exception. The job is demanding and challenging. Beginning salaries are high, but in most cases they plateau, creating frustration for experienced nurses. Hazards abound because nurses are exposed to infectious diseases, chemicals, and violence, and the hours can be long.

Nursing Is a Demanding Profession

Nursing is a physically and psychologically demanding profession, and the nursing shortage has increased these demands. Fewer nurses mean more clients per nurse and less time per client. Nurses are forced to work overtime, adding to their exhaustion, and the decrease in client contact creates frustration because nurses can't do what they were educated to do.

Shift work can cause adverse physical and psychological effects, including disruption in your biological rhythm, sleep disorders, health problems, diminished work performance, job dissatisfaction, and social isolation. Nurses spend much of their day on their feet, causing foot, leg, and back problems for many. Back problems can also arise from all the lifting that is required. Most of the latter problems can be minimized with good shoes, suitable hosiery, and proper body mechanics.

Nurses are there when bad things happen to people. Cancer, accidents, mental illness, violence, and death are but a few of the issues that nurses deal with on a regular basis. They also work closely with clients' families, and they often need to make critical decisions and deal with ethical dilemmas. While it's rewarding to help people through these tough times, it can also be psychologically draining. Unlike other healthcare professionals, nurses have an intimate relationship with clients, caring for their most personal needs—bathing them, helping them use the toilet. Nurses are also with hospitalized clients around the clock. Working with people at some of the most vulnerable moments of their lives makes some workdays difficult, and nurses must take steps to assure that this stress doesn't affect their professional, personal, or family life.

Potentially Dangerous Work Conditions

Nursing can be hazardous to your health, especially nursing in hospitals, clinics, long-term care facilities, and home care where nurses may come in contact with infectious diseases, toxic chemicals, potent medications, and hazardous waste. Nurses must observe strict standardized guidelines to protect themselves and others from disease and other dangers, including accidental needle sticks and radiation.

Emergency nurses care for victims and offenders of violent crimes, thus making emergency rooms dangerous places to work at times. Some emergency departments have round-the-clock police protection. All nurses work with victims of family violence—child abuse, intimate partner violence, and elder abuse, and all work with clients who have psychiatric disorders, even if that is not their primary diagnosis. Violence has become a concern in healthcare. But while the exposure to violence presents a disadvantage to nurses, it also has become an opportunity in the form of a relatively new specialty, forensic nursing.

Salary Ceilings

The starting salaries are excellent, but seasoned nurses often hit a ceiling where the only salary increase they receive is a cost-of-living raise.

Long Hours

Working just two or three days a week sounds fantastic, but 12-hour shifts can take their toll. Eight-hour shifts can grow into 10 or 12 with overtime, which may help financially but can be exhausting physically, especially if the overtime is mandated.

The pros and cons of nursing extend into the student experience. The life of a nursing student is quite different from most other majors. Time is at a premium, and practicum experiences can be life-changing, for both client and student.

NURSING NOTES

Content with Compromise, by Isabel Roitman

I live in a house filled with 23 girls. Of the 23, 22 of them are not nursing students. To say the least, I am a minority. My life is a little different than theirs.

When the other girls wake up to the noise of pans clattering and the toaster ticking, they remember it's just me, making breakfast at 6:30 A.M. before my clinical rotation at the nursing home. They go back to sleep; I shove my half-cooked egg sandwich into my mouth and run out the door. I start my car, pick up my friend Rachel, another nursing student, and we make our way to the nursing home, rushing to make it in the sliding doors by 7:00 A.M. We meet our patient and by 9:00 A.M., my partner and I have given our patient a complete bed bath and fed her breakfast. By 10:00 A.M. we have dressed our patient. By 11:00 A.M., all the students meet in the conference room of the nursing home to debrief with our instructor. We share funny stories, sad stories, and shocking stories from the day; we reflect on our actions; and we give each other support. We say good-bye to our patients, leave the facility, and head over to campus for our next class that begins at 1:00 P.M. Although we'd all love to go back and curl up in our warm, comfortable beds, we continue our day. But then I remember that jumping on the college life bandwagon and skipping a class is not an option for a student prepping for the nursing field. It's not an option because what I learn today will save a life tomorrow.

There are times when I wake up and wish I could sleep in or wish I could stay up later chatting and laughing with my friends about nonsense. Sometimes I even wish I could forget the painful cries I've heard at the nursing home. Yet it never seems to escape me the grateful smile my patient had as we repositioned her helpless body, or the smile one of my friends had after I cleaned a cut of his, stopped the bleeding, and bandaged it. I also then remember why I decided to join this crazy life in the first place. Like the well-known poet and musician, Niccolo Machiavelli, once wrote, "the end justifies the means." I realize that my journey to become a nurse, although a great compromise at times, will eventually lead me to my dream.

THE NURSING EXPERIENCE

The best way to find out if nursing is for you is to shadow a nurse. Contact your school of interest and ask if they allow it. High school students can also attend *nurse camp* at a local college and spend a few days immersed in the nursing experience. Nurse camp allows you to practice on computerized mannequins and use nursing equipment. You'll also get to talk to students and instructors, which gives you a chance to ask questions about your potential career.

Nurse Camp

■ Attend nursing classes taught by nursing faculty.

■ Learn about the student experience from nursing students.

■ Learn and practice skills in a nursing laborator.y

■ Utilize computerized mannequins that simulate real patient illnesses.

■ Observe nurses in a hospital unit.

■ Find out about nursing specialties.

If time or distance prohibits you from firsthand experience, or if you'd rather read about nursing before jumping in, here is an inside look at the nursing experience. The skills noted here are by no means all-inclusive. They were chosen to give you an insight into the world of nursing, and are intended to give you a brief overview, not to teach you the skill. As they say on television, nurses are professionals—don't try these skills on your own.

Health Assessment

As the first component of the nursing process, assessment encompasses a number of skills that let you do some detective work. Nurses assess clients' four domains: physical, psychological, social, and spiritual. Physical health involves basic functions such as breathing, eating, sleeping, and walking, while psychological health involves a person's intellect, self-concept, emotions, and behavior. Social health encompasses the client's relationship with family, friends, coworkers, and society, and spiritual health refers to a person's meaning of life, attitudes toward moral conduct, and belief in a higher power. Nurses consider all these dimensions when performing a comprehensive assessment.

Assessments include both subjective and objective data. Subjective data, also called history, are the symptoms, feelings, perceptions, and other information that the client states and validates. Objective data, also called physical, are the signs directly measured, observed, and felt by the nurse. Nurses need to be able to assess all types of clients, and to modify their assessment to meet the client's age and health status. Children are not just small adults; their bodies are different, and they don't have an adult's level of understanding. Thus, nurses learn skills to both assess children and communicate with them. Older adults require skill modification as well, as do critically ill persons. You need to move faster if a client is in a life-threatening situation, and you need to alter the order of your assessment. Nurses thus learn both assessment skills and assessment modifications. However, before they assess, nurses initiate the nurse-client relationship and discuss confidentiality.

Nurse-Client Relationship

The nurse-client relationship is a helping relationship that differs from social relationships. It focuses on the client, is goal directed, and has defined parameters. The nurse-client relationship begins with the orientation phase, which consists of introductions and an agreement between the nurse and client about their roles and responsibilities. The second phase is the working phase, during which the nurse and client participate together in the client's care. The nurse acts as the client's advocate, caring for his or her physical and emotional healthcare needs. The final phase is termination, which is the closure of the relationship. Here the nurse reviews the client's aspects of care and how they have dealt with physical and emotional responses. Termination is also the time for discharge planning.

Confidentiality

Confidentiality requires that client information remain private between the client and the healthcare team. No one else is entitled to the client's information unless the client signs a consent for release of information. Nurses need to tell clients about their right to confidentiality, and they need to avoid discussing clients outside the clinical setting. Telling friends or family about clients violates the client's right to confidentiality and could result in disciplinary action for the nurse.

In respect to confidentiality, nurses are required to adhere to the Health Privacy Rule of the Health Insurance Portability and Accountability Act (HIPAA). HIPAA was enacted to ensure health insurance coverage after leaving an employer and to improve the efficiency and effectiveness of health care-related electronic transactions. The Department of Health and Human Services (DHHS) developed the Standards for Privacy of Individually Identifiable Health Information, better known as the HIPAA Privacy Rule. The privacy rule regulates how certain groups or persons can use and disclose individually identifiable health information. The privacy rule:

▶ grants client patients more control over their own health information, and sets boundaries on the use and release of health records.

▶ enables patients to make informed choices and to know how, when, and for whom their protected health information is used.

▶ limits the release of protected health information to the minimum necessary for the purposes of the disclosure.

▶ establishes safeguards that most healthcare providers must achieve to protect client health information, and allows civil and criminal penalties to be imposed on those who violate the rule.

▶ allows for disclosure of protected health information for public health, safety, and law enforcement purposes.

Subjective Data

Once nurses establish the nurse-client relationship and discuss confidentiality, they are ready to begin assessment (even though nurses actually begin their assessment when they first see and hear the client). Nurses first collect subjective data using therapeutic communication techniques. Communication is a powerful tool, and therapeutic communication techniques are some of the most important skills in a nurse's toolbox.

Examples of Therapeutic Communication Techniques

■ *Broad opening statements* allow clients to set the direction of the interview: "Where would you like to begin?"

■ *Active listening* is more than hearing; it involves the nurse's ability to focus on and decode what the client is saying.

■ *Open-ended questions* require more than a "yes" or "no" answer: "How would you describe your pain?"

■ *Focusing* helps to keep the client on topic: "You were telling me about your heart problem; can you tell me more about it?"

■ *General leads* encourage the client to continue: "And then?"

■ *Silence* may be the best response. It slows the pace of the interview and allows the client to reflect on his or her feelings.

Once nurses establish the relationship and confidentiality, they begin the interview, usually asking about the chief complaint, which is the reason why the client sought healthcare. The nurse then obtains the client's health history, which includes medications, allergies, nutrition, elimination, sleep patterns, hospitalizations, injuries, and family health. Nurses then ask questions about each body system—for example, they will ask about breathing problems and coughing to assess the respiratory system. Since nurses use a multidimensional model, they will also ask about the client's psychological, social, and spiritual health. The main purpose of the history is to focus the physical assessment, but the history also provides insight into the client's healthcare teaching needs, which may include nutritional counseling or smoking cessation.

Vital Signs

At some point during or immediately after collecting subjective data, nurses assess vital signs: blood pressure, temperature, pulse, respirations, and what is now called the fifth vital sign, pain, which is discussed later in this chapter. Vital signs reflect the client's overall health and changes can indicate serious illness. Therefore, nurses need to know both technique and interpretation. For example, you need to know how to use different types of thermometers, as well as know that an increase in temperature can signify problems such as infection, increased stress, heat stroke, and some types of cancer. Pulse and respirations are more than just numbers. Did you know there are 17 pulse sites? Both pulse and respiration have characteristics such as rhythm and quality, and respiration characteristics also include depth. A slow pulse (under 60 beats per minute in an adult) is called *bradycardia*, while a rapid one (greater than 100 beats per minute in an adult) is *tachycardia*. *Dyspnea* means difficult breathing.

Blood pressure may be measured directly with a catheter placed in an artery, a measurement monitored by critical care nurses. But most nurses use the indirect and more commonly known method, using a stethoscope and sphygmomanometer (blood pressure cuff). For those people with hard to hear blood pressures, nurses use the Doppler method, an electronic system similar to home blood pressure machines. Blood pressure assessment takes skill. An overly wide cuff can cause a falsely low reading, while a cuff that's too narrow can cause the reading to be falsely high. Readings are typically documented in fraction form, with one number over another. The top number is the systolic blood pressure; the bottom, the diastolic. Normal adult blood pressure is 120/80.

Measurements

If you're health conscious, you know about measuring height, weight, and basal metabolic index. But you'll go beyond the bathroom scale as a nurse— you'll learn to use chair and bed scales, as well as standardized height and weight charts. More importantly, you will learn how weight provides important information about clients' nutritional and hydration status. Weight can also help evaluate treatment response, particularly in clients who are receiving diuretics (water pills).

According to the Centers for Disease Control and Prevention (CDC), body mass index (BMI), a number calculated from a person's weight and height, is a reliable indicator of body fatness for people. While there is a mathematical equation to determine BMI, most nurses rely on a BMI calculator, such as the one on the National Institutes of Health's website: www.nhlbisupport.com/bmi. BMI is used to screen, not diagnose, weight problems, using standardized weight status categories that are the same for all male and female adults 20 and older.

BMI Categories

- Underweight   <18.5
- Normal weight   18.5–24.9
- Overweight   25–29.9
- Obesity   BMI of 30 or greater

Physical Assessment

Physical assessment involves using your senses to obtain objective data from clients. The physical boils down to four assessment techniques: inspection, palpation, percussion, and auscultation. Inspection involves careful observation of behaviors and physical features, such as inspecting the skin for rashes. Palpation is the use of the fingers and hands to gather assessment information through touch. The nurse palpates the abdomen to see if the liver is enlarged. Percussion involves listening for specific sounds while tapping the fingers on certain body areas. The nurse can percuss the bladder to determine if it is filled with urine. Auscultation is the listening for the sounds of movement within the body using a stethoscope. The nurse auscultates the lungs to assess the quality of air movement.

All nurses perform some level of physical assessment, but complete head-to-toe assessment is usually reserved for registered nurses who attained the baccalaureate and/or a higher level of education. Bachelor-prepared nurses take a course in health assessment, where they learn both technique and interpretation. They use their assessment skills as part of the nursing process. Advanced practice nurses, prepared at the master's or doctoral level, use advanced physical assessment skills to make diagnoses.

Client Hygiene

Nurses assist clients with their most basic needs: eating, toileting, and sleeping. Nurses help patients eat regular meals or special diets, and they feed patients through devices, including nasogastric (nose to stomach) and gastrostomy (directly into the stomach through the skin) tubes. Nurses certainly handle their share of bedpans and urinals, but they also maintain elimination by inserting and monitoring urinary catheters, and care for ostomies, surgical openings created to allow clients to urinate or stool through an opening in the abdomen. Healthy sleep begins with a comfortable bed, and nurses develop bed-making skills that allow them to make beds while clients occupy them.

Infection Control

Infection control involves hand hygiene, preparing sterile fields, and using standardized precautions. You're probably wondering why something as everyday (hopefully, more often!) as handwashing is listed as a skill. But proper handwashing is the most important defense against spreading infection, and once you learn proper handwashing, you'll never go back to your old way again. Hand hygiene also includes the proper use of alcohol-based rubs, which can substitute for handwashing in some situations.

Sterile fields provide aseptic (germ-free) workspace. Nurses prepare sterile fields to dress wounds and perform sterile procedures. Standardized precautions prevent the spread of infectious diseases through the use of personal protective equipment (PPE) that includes gloves, masks, gowns/aprons and eye shields that form barriers between the nurse and client. The type of PPE used varies based on the type of exposure anticipated or category of isolation determined by CDC guidelines. Nurses also use *standard precautions* for all clients, in all settings, regardless of suspected or confirmed infectious status. These precautions are based on the principle that all blood, body fluids, secretions, excretions except sweat, nonintact skin, and mucous membranes may contain transmissible infectious agents. The precautions include: hand hygiene; use of gloves, gown, mask, eye protection, or face shield, depending on the anticipated exposure; and safe injection practices. For some procedures (e.g., performing venipuncture), only gloves may be needed; during other interactions (e.g., intubation), use of gloves, gown, and face shield or mask and goggles is necessary.

Specimen Collection

Specimen collection aids in the screening and diagnosing of illnesses, directing of treatment, and monitoring of progress. Nurses collect a number of specimens, but the most common are blood, urine, and stool. They regularly perform glucose monitoring on diabetic clients, check urine for specific gravity, blood, and bacteria, and check stool for occult (not visible) blood. Pediatric nurses regularly swab children's throats to test for strep throat, while women's health nurses may collect specimens during a gynecological exam to assess for sexually transmitted diseases and cervical cancer. Forensic nurses collect specimens for DNA testing.

Medication Administration

Medication administration is a common but crucial function that requires defined skills and considerable knowledge about pharmacology and clients' health status. Nurses need to know drugs' generic and trade names, classification, action, indications, dosage, delivery method, side effects, precautions, contraindications, effects on laboratory tests, drug-to-drug interactions, nursing considerations, and client teaching needs. Here is some of what nurses need to know about aspirin, a seemingly simple medication:

Generic name: Aspirin and acetylsalicylic acid.

Trade names: At least 18, including ASA, Bayer Aspirin, and Ecotrin.

Classification: Nonopioid analgesic (pain reliever) and antipyretic (fever reducer). (Nurses need to know that aspirin is also used as an anti-inflammatory and anticlotting medication.)

Action: Aspirin is thought to relieve pain by inhibiting prostaglandin and other substances that sensitize pain receptors. It may reduce fever by acting on the hypothalamic heat-regulating center and may exert an anti-inflammatory response by inhibiting prostaglandin and other substances. Low doses of aspirin seem to interfere with clotting by keeping a platelet-aggregating substance from forming.

Indications and Dosages: For mild pain and fever in adults and children over 11 years old: 325 to 650 milligrams every four hours as needed. For the inflammation of arthritis in adults: 2.4 to 3.6 grams daily in divided doses, followed by a maintenance dose of 3.2 to 6.0 grams daily in divided doses. To reduce the risk of stroke in adults: 50 to 325 milligrams daily.

Delivery method: Orally (tablets or chewing gum) or rectally (suppositories)

Side effects: Tinnitus (ringing in ears), hearing loss, nausea, gastrointestinal bleeding, upset stomach, prolonged bleeding time, leukopenia (low white blood cell count), thrombocytopenia (low platelets), hepatitis, rash, bruising, hives, angioedema (allergic skin disease), Reye's syndrome (potentially fatal disease in children), and hypersensitivity reactions.

Precautions: There are multiple precautions, including use with caution in persons with impaired kidney function, vitamin K deficiency, or low platelet count.

Contraindications: Aspirin is contraindicated in clients who are hypersensitive to the drug and persons with certain gastrointestinal problems or bleeding disorders.

Effects on laboratory tests: May interfere with urine glucose analysis.

Drug-to-drug interactions: There are several, including: anticoagulants (increases risk of bleeding), oral antidiabetics (may increase low blood sugar effect), and antacids (decrease aspirin effect). Some herbal drugs interact with aspirin, increasing the risk for bleeding.

Nursing considerations: Enteric-coated and slow-release tablets should not be used for acute pain or fever because these preparations are slowly absorbed.

Client teaching: Some over-the-counter (OTC) preparations contain aspirin; read labels carefully to avoid overdosing. Alcohol may increase the risk of bleeding, and caffeine may increase aspirin absorption. Clients on low salt diets should be aware that buffered aspirin contains 553 milligrams of sodium. Because there are so many drug-to-drug interactions, clients taking prescription or herbal medications should speak to their healthcare provider before taking aspirin or OTC products containing aspirin.

Medications are administered orally, rectally, vaginally, intravenously, and topically, as well as under the tongue and via injection. Nurses also administer eye, ear, and nose preparations. When administering medications, nurses adhere to the client "Rights to Medication Administration": right medication, given to the right patient, in the right dosage, through the right route, at the right time. Additional suggested rights are giving the medication for the right reason and ensuring the right documentation. Nurses also assure that clients understand their responsibilities about their medications, especially if the client will be responsible for self-administration.

Pain Management

Nurses ensure clients' comfort in a number of ways such as fluffing a pillow or holding a client's hand. But pain management is the most important and complex comfort mechanism. No two people experience pain the same way since people have different perceptions and responses to pain, necessitating careful assessment. When assessing pain, nurses consider location, intensity, quality, and temporal pattern. Superficial pain emanates from the skin or just below it, allowing the client to easily demonstrate where it comes from. Internal pain, however, may not be localized and may actually be felt in an area distant from the affected organ. For example, a patient with a heart problem may feel the pain in his left arm. Clients may describe their pain as mild to severe or on a scale of 0 to 10, with zero being no pain and 10 being the worst pain they ever experienced. Quality refers to how the pain feels, such as sharp, dull, or stabbing. Clients may find an analogy easier to describe their pain and use phrases such as "like a knife went through me" or "being hit with a hammer." Pain from a heart attack may be described as "It feels like an elephant is sitting on my chest." Temporal pattern stands for when the pain started (onset) and how long it lasted (duration). Clients may have pain all the time, for one occasion, or intermittently, as pain may be acute or chronic.

Nurses manage pain through physical, cognitive, behavioral, and pharmacological therapies. Physical pain relief includes repositioning, hygiene, and cutaneous stimulation. Repositioning a bedridden client can relieve pain from pressure spots, while simple cleaning can decrease discomfort from irritated skin. Cutaneous stimulation refers to heat, cold, massage, vibration, and the application of pain-relieving ointments. All help to relax and distract clients and create an analgesic (pain relieving) effect. Cognitive techniques work well with certain types of pain. Distraction (looking at comforting pictures or listening to music) helps with brief periods of pain, such as those experienced when undergoing a procedure. Guided imagery can minimize pain or act as a pain substitute, while anticipatory guidance teaches clients how to minimize pain before it happens. Behavioral techniques such as relaxation and meditation can enable clients to feel a sense of control over their pain. Pharmacological pain management relies on analgesic medications, some of which are potent and highly regulated narcotics, requiring the nurse to monitor for adverse effects such as respiratory problems, tolerance, dependence, and addiction. Nurses administer analgesics and evaluate their effectiveness.

Treatments

Nursing interventions involve numerous client treatments, with the more common ones being intravenous therapy, wound care, oxygen administration, tracheotomy care, and cast and traction care. Given that nurses perform these treatments regularly, and given that these treatments require considerable knowledge and skill, they are focal points in basic nursing education. Therefore, you will learn about them in class, practice them in the nursing laboratory, and most likely be tested on your performance of them.

Intravenous (IV) therapy is the infusion of fluid into a vein to correct fluid and/or electrolyte imbalance or to deliver nutrition, medications, or blood products. The treatment goal may be maintenance, replacement, palliation, or a combination. Nurses administer and monitor IV therapy in hospitals, outpatient settings, long-term care facilities, and client homes, and most nurses also initiate IV therapy by performing a venipuncture, the insertion of a needle or catheter into a vein. This method is common for short-term IV therapy. When clients warrant long-term IV therapy, concentrated medications or total parenteral nutrition (nutrition via IV), physicians typically insert other devices, such as central venous access devices or peripherally inserted central catheters (PICC). These catheters can cause more complications, thus needing more intricate nursing care and monitoring. For all IV therapy, careful monitoring promotes adequate administration of treatment and prevention of complications, such as catheter blockage, infection, phlebitis (inflammation of the vein), fluid overload, and infiltration (needle or catheter slips out of the vein and leaks fluid into the tissue).

Wound care involves numerous principles, including infection control. The skin acts as the body's largest organ, providing protective, sensory, and regulatory functions. Therefore breaks in the skin's integrity can interfere with these functions and cause problems. Nurses refer to breaks as wounds. Accidental wounds may be caused by burns or trauma, while intentional wounds are created by surgical intervention and usually called incisions. Both types of wounds may require nursing care. Nurses assess wounds to determine their stage of healing and to monitor them for complications. They also ascertain clients' risk for delayed wound healing, such as allergies, skin conditions, malnutrition, diabetes mellitus, infection, impaired circulation, immuosuppression, obesity, and stress. Wound care may also involve medication administration, skin care, and dressing changes. Clients with significant wounds, such as those caused by second and third degree burns, may need more intensive management.

Respiratory treatments vary from helping a client deep breathe and cough to working with mechanical ventilators. Most nurses promote normal respiratory function regardless of their specialty. Hospital nurses administer oxygen, community nurses screen for tuberculosis, and school nurses teach children about the hazards of smoking. Nurses use incentive spirometry, a device that encourages deep breathing, to prevent respiratory complications. They provide chest physiotherapy to clear excessive mucous in clients with cystic fibrosis, chronic obstructive pulmonary disease, and pneumonia. Chest physiotherapy primarily consists of: percussion, striking the chest wall with cupped hands or an electronic percussor; vibration, using hands or a mechanical jacket to vibrate the chest; and postural drainage, positioning the client in manners that use gravity to move secretions. Nurses may also provide medications via the respiratory system, using aerosol treatment or handheld inhalers.

For clients with lung disease, oxygen helps eliminate dyspnea and improve comfort. For some of these clients, meticulous oxygen therapy saves their lives. Oxygen is considered a medication and thus warrants a prescription or physician's order that determines the flow or concentration. It is safe when used properly, but potentially harmful if misused. Therefore, nurses need to know the principles of oxygen therapy, as well as how to use the mechanisms of delivery, such as nasal tubing, oxygen masks, and oxygen tents.

Mechanical ventilators provide artificial respiration for clients who cannot breathe on their own. These machines were once only found in intensive care units, but now are used on general hospital units, rehabilitation centers, and even home care, adding them to the list of equipment that nurses need to know. Ventilators require frequent monitoring and knowledge about their use and alarm systems.

Clients requiring long-term mechanical ventilation, as well as clients with certain health problems, may require a tracheotomy, in which an artificial airway is implanted into the trachea below the vocal cords. *Tracheotomy care* decreases the risk of infection and obstruction. Nurses clean the tubing and care for the incision. Nurses also assess the site for signs of infection, and they assist the client in communicating and with body image concerns.

Accidents are common, especially in children, and many result in broken bones that need *casts*, *traction*, or *other devices* to help them heal. Most injuries are minor, but significant injuries can immobilize clients for quite some time. Immobility can result in muscle weakness and wasting, muscle shortening (contractures) and joint pain, increased cardiac workload, drop in blood pressure when going from lying to standing, blood clots, lung problems, loss of appetite, osteoporosis, impaired immunity, urinary and bowel problems, and pressure sores. Immobility can also impact on the client's sleep, self-concept, relationships, and sexuality. Nurses thus must be aware of all these potential complications, how to assess them, how to prevent them, and what to do if they develop. The nursing process applies to clients in casts and other devices. Nurses assess the affected area to assure that there is no impairment in circulation, nerve conduction, and skin integrity. They also assure that the device is functioning properly and assist the client with ambulation when needed. Assisted ambulation may mean that the nurse teaches the client how to walk with crutches, a cane, or a walker.

Perioperative Care

You may have no plans to ever set foot in an operating room after graduation, but chances are that you will spend some time there doing a clinical rotation when you are a nursing student. Many illnesses and injuries require surgery, which may be minor or major, planned or unplanned, and may involve one body part or a whole system. Surgical procedures may be performed in a hospital, physician's office or clinic, or an ambulatory surgical center, and many surgical procedures create stress, necessitating physical and psychological adaptation for the client and family. Surgery can affect activity, nutrition, temperature regulation, urinary and bowel function, sleep, body image, and relationships. Most postoperative clients will experience pain, and most are at risk for bleeding and infection. Client recovery commands knowledgeable and skillful nursing care, referred to as perioperative care when it encompasses care before, during, and after surgery.

Preoperatively, nurses perform a comprehensive assessment to look for risk factors that can contribute to complications from the surgery or the anesthesia. This assessment includes a history and physical assessment, as well as monitoring laboratory tests such as blood studies (including type and cross match in case transfusion is needed), urinalysis, electrocardiogram, and chest x-ray. Nurses also teach clients what to expect during the surgical phases and how they can participate in their own recovery. Surgical preparation can be extensive as some clients needing IVs, medications, stomach decompression, bowel cleansing, and operative site cleansing and shaving. During surgery, nurses may act as either a scrub nurse who provides the surgeon with equipment or a circulating nurse who protects the client's safety and health needs. Operating room nurses also assure that equipment functions properly. During the postoperative phase, which begins when the client enters the recovery facility, nurses perform continuous monitoring to detect possible complications and assure the client's comfort.

Client Teaching

Give a man a fish; you have fed him for today. Teach a man to fish; and you have fed him for a lifetime.

—Author unknown

Learning empowers clients to manage their healthcare problems and possibly achieve a higher level of wellness. Nurses frequently teach clients and reinforce information from other healthcare providers. Hospital nurses teach illness management; school nurses teach nutrition; occupational nurses teach work safety; psychiatric nurses teach coping skills; and forensic nurses teach about violence prevention.

Hospitals seem like great places for illness teaching, but the stress of illness and hospitalization can hinder learning, creating challenges for the nurse. Added to this is the increasing knowledge level of today's healthcare consumer, thanks to the Internet. Clients can google practically every disease and health topic known to mankind and find a plethora of information. Unfortunately, clients may not be able to differentiate fact from fiction because some web sites provide inaccurate information. To meet these challenges, nurses apply the nursing process to client teaching and begin with assessment of clients' learning needs. Nurses first analyze the client's baseline knowledge with broad opening statements like, "Tell me what you know about your diabetes." This gives the nurse someplace to begin. Nurses next assess the client's health and cultural beliefs as well as their language skills, since these factors can impact on the teaching-learning process. For example, some cultures utilize folk medicines and nurses need to accept client beliefs and integrate them into the teaching-learning process. Nurses identify client priorities and motivation. For example, a postoperative client with newly diagnosed high cholesterol may be more interested in learning how to get back to work than learning about a low fat diet. Nurses can teach this client about his priority need and still develop a discharge teaching plan that creates an opening for him to later learn about the diet. Finally, nurses assess the client's literacy level and physical state. The client's ability to read and write guides how the teaching will proceed, and the client's physical state determines the client's ability to process information. Pain and other issues may diminish concentration.

Once nurses complete their assessment and diagnose the client's knowledge deficit, they identify outcomes, then create a teaching plan and implement it. Most nurses teach clients on a one-to-one basis, using teaching aids such as pamphlets, DVDs, and models; others teach client groups. The latter is typical of nurses who teach clients to care for their diabetes, chronic lung disease, or heart problems.

Nurses teach about all illnesses, but they also teach about health, helping clients to attain and maintain an optimal level of wellness. Health teaching spans the lifecycle, requiring nurses to know development. Infants are not ready for formal education, so nurses teach parents and encourage them to provide their infants with safe, developmentally enhancing toys. Toddlers and preschoolers learn though play. Toddlers like to imitate and preschoolers ask lots of questions. Preschoolers are usually proud of their accomplishments and thus respond well to teaching that is accompanied by praise and stickers. School-age children enjoy learning about their bodies, and can understand cause and effect, allowing nurses to help them set goals. Adolescents strive for independence and appreciate having some control over their healthcare. Adult learners respond well to straightforward teaching that allows them to apply their newfound knowledge immediately. Knowledge does not decrease with age unless affected by illness, and older adults usually have as much to teach as they do to learn. Healthy lifestyle teaching pertains to the whole lifespan, thus nurses continuously teach about proper nutrition, normal sleep and elimination patterns, exercise, and stress management. But each developmental stage presents with its own health needs as exemplified in the following table.

Examples of Wellness Topics Taught by Nurses

Client Group	Healthcare Topics
Parents of infants	Safe sleep, shaken-baby syndrome prevention, weaning, teething
Parents of toddlers	Temper tantrums, toilet training, safety, discipline
Preschoolers and their parents	Hand washing, tooth brushing, healthy snacks, nightmares, and night terrors
School-age children	Bicycle safety, obesity prevention and management, tobacco prevention, bullying, puberty
Adolescents	Safe dating practices, contraception, driving safety, peer pressure, drug and alcohol dangers, acne
Women	Breast self-examination, prenatal classes, Lamaze, breast-feeding, menopause
Men	Testicular self-examination, sports injury prevention and management, prostate health

Counseling

Nurses do not provide psychiatric therapy, unless they are advanced practice psychiatric nurses, but they do counsel clients. Nurses counsel clients as they adapt to changes in life, body image, role performance, self-esteem, and personal identity. They counsel families about relationships and the changes in those relationships, including divorce. Nurses counsel about loss and grief. Loss can be anything from empty nest syndrome to the death of a loved one, and grieving manifests differently in every client. Nurses counsel by helping people identify their strengths and mobilizing their resources. They teach coping skills, stress management, and problem solving, and they enable clients to work through the stages of grief.

Informatics

Informatics evolved over the last four decades to assist nurses in all areas of nursing practice. Thus today's nurses need to be as savvy with a computer as they are with a ventilator. While this field has become a nursing specialty in its own right, most nurses work with some form of computerized system. Computerized systems aid in assessment because many programs prompt nurses to ask clients further questions as the nurses enter data. The program then analyzes the assessment data to generate possible nursing diagnoses and potential interventions. Computerized nurses' notes sort and print out client data, including vital signs, medications, and treatments to make documentation more efficient and accurate. If you're concerned that you lack the technology skills to be a nurse, don't worry. Most nursing programs have resources to help turn the novice computer phobic into a proficient computer techie.

SUITABILITY TEST

After weighing the pros and cons and getting psyched about the nursing experience, you know you want to be a nurse. Now you're probably asking yourself, "Do I have what it takes to be a nurse?" Answer the following questions.

1. Are you a critical thinker? No matter what specialty you choose, nursing requires lifelong learning and the ability to think on your feet.

2. Can you handle the physical demands? You'll do a lot of lifting and standing as a nursing student. But you can choose a less physically demanding job, such as psychiatric or school nursing, when you graduate.

3. Do you have a strong stomach? Nurses handle sputum, vomit, urine, stool, and other unpleasant excrement. Again, you can opt for a less messy specialty after graduation, but you'll still get your gloved hands dirty as a student.

4. Do you have people skills? While there are a few nursing jobs with little people contact, most require an ability to communicate with others. You only need the ability to get along with others to get started; you'll learn therapeutic communication during your nursing education.

5. Are you flexible? Things change quickly when you work with clients. You may face unexpected admissions, sudden changes in your clients' status, a disaster drill, or equipment failure. Regardless of what happens, you need to be able to go with the flow.

6. Are you patient? It may take several minutes to feed a client a bowl of soup or to get someone out of bed after surgery. You need to be able to exercise patience, even though you have a long list of other things to do.

7. Do you like working with a team? Today's healthcare system is just that, a system, and nurses are a critical component of the interdisciplinary team. All nurses work with others, including those in independent practice who still collaborate with other professionals.

8. Are you in love with learning? Healthcare changes rapidly and nursing education is lifelong. In fact, many states require that nurses complete 10 to 30 hours of continuing education to renew their licenses.

9. Do you have a sense of humor? This isn't mandatory, but it will help you get through the tough times!

10. Do you want to help others? If so, you can learn to manage questions 1 through 6.

If you answered "yes" to most of these questions, you have nursing potential. If you answered "yes" to all of them, what are you waiting for? Talk to a career counselor or a nursing program advisor.

Now that you think you found your dream career, other questions may come to your mind. You're not alone. Many people ask these same questions when considering nursing.

1. Am I too old to be a nurse? Some people enter nursing after retiring from another career. As long as you can handle the physical and psychological challenges of nursing, you're never too old.

2. What if I do poorly on exams? You will have to take exams throughout school, as well as your licensing exam (NCLEX). If you have difficulty, talk to an advisor before applying for admission. Ask about their academic support system. Most schools have personnel to help you with your learning needs.

3. What if I'm bad at math? You do need basic math skills. Brush up before you start your nursing program, or ask an advisor about math tutors or remedial courses. Most programs allow calculators, so make sure to purchase one before you start. Cell phones are not allowed during exams (to prevent text-cheating) or on client units (because of confidentiality), so get an old-fashioned pocket calculator.

4. How do I know if I have a strong stomach? If you have gotten this far in life without getting your hands dirty, ask to shadow a hospital nurse for a day. Confidentiality rules will limit what you can see, but you should be able to see, hear, and smell enough to find out the extent of your stomach's strength.

5. Can I be a nurse if I have a disability? Nurses do need to be able to perform certain essential skills. If you are concerned about your disability interfering with your career goals, talk to an advisor. There may be special equipment or circumstances to help you meet those goals, and nursing programs provide reasonable accommodations to

students with disabilities as required under the Americans with Disabilities Act of 1990.

Only you can make the final decision to become a nurse. But you don't have to reach that decision alone. Besides seeking professional career advice, talk to nurses. Ask them about the advantages and disadvantages. Most importantly, ask them, if they had to start over, would they still be a nurse?

NURSING NOTES

In Appreciation for What We Have, by Jacquelynn Pasamba

At the time I was a junior and abroad in the Dominican Republic, I was working as a student nurse along with my fellow classmates, a group of overworked, overcaffeinated, overstressed, and sleep deprived library rat inhabitants. We were a team of six under the supervision and guidance of one very patient professor. That particular day we began the morning in the Labor and Delivery unit at the medical center in San Pedro de Macoraris.

I will never forget the incessant piercing screaming, but even more, the smell of stagnant air—a remarkable mixture of emesis, blood, sweat, and everything in between. Picture a ward with different subsections and rooms separated by walls and doors accordingly, but each filled with as many beds as possible. It is as if the architect engineered the space planning to keep a free flow of movement yet a distinction of rooms in mind. However, the inhabitants had the complete opposite intentions, displayed by their utter disregard for patient privacy with the lack of curtains between beds and lack of patient gowns resulting in an abundance of unnecessary nudity. A lot of the major differences between American and Dominican hospitals and care are rooted in the same necessary evil: funding and lack thereof. The lack of medications, equipment, and resources as mundane as electricity and water—which many Americans take for granted—made us fully comprehend the pure novelty and genius of hand sanitizer dispensers scattered among numerous if not all hospitals in the United States. In addition, we realized the importance of resources such as bedsheets or food trays and quickly learned to appreciate them.

The delivery room was also dimly lit, crowded, smelly, and cold—cold, from the actual appearance of objects to people. The doctors and nurses wanted to get in and

and out; everything was a procedure, routine. Patients were categorized versus seen or treated as individuals, people. For instance, none of the patients had identification bands. Only one doctor asked the patient how she was doing, interestingly only at the end of the delivery.

We witnessed two women giving birth adjacent to each other with literally no barrier between the two mothers, not even a curtain. One woman gave life, the other saw what could have been. The doctors examined both babies next to each other. It was a memorable and defining experience. Life and death so close in proximity, literally side by side, within arm's reach. One infant gained color and heat as time progressed, while the other turned darker and colder. The face of the mother when she realized her loss haunts me to this day. She wasn't informed until the end of both deliveries. She was alone in the room with the delivering nurse, still lying in the lithotomy position. Her sheer terror, grief, yet loneliness and emptiness when one stared into her bulging deep brown eyes painted on her blank face; her gasping for air and immediate demand to see her baby, her little girl.

As distressing and heartbreaking as this memory is to me, I've learned to take the positives from each experience. The most remarkable and admirable aspect of the Dominicans I encountered was their ability to find happiness in the most distressing situations. Regardless of their circumstance, whether it be financial, physical, mental, or all of the above, everyone was able to crack a joke, laugh, and enjoy life. When I confessed this thought to my professor she responded, "That's because they don't know anything else." In hindsight I like to think of it as, "It's because of everything they do know."

CHAPTER three

ENTRY-LEVEL EDUCATION

THE FIRST step toward becoming a nurse is selecting the educational program that's right for you. You need to consider whether you want to be a practical nurse or a registered nurse, and if you choose registered nursing, you must decide on whether to obtain a diploma, associate degree, or baccalaureate degree. If you already have a baccalaurcate or higher degree, your options increase, allowing you to add accelerated programs into your options. But there is more to this decision than choosing levels. You need to consider educational costs and time commitment.

CHOOSING AN ENTRY-LEVEL NURSING PROGRAM

Choosing an entry-level nursing education program can be quite confusing, even after you've decided between becoming an RN or LPN. Most schools have web sites that provide information about their programs, including course information and costs. This section helps you understand the differences among the various entry-level programs, which for RNs vary from hospital-based programs to those at the master's degree level.

State Board Approval and National Accreditation of Nursing Education

Before choosing any nursing program, make sure that it is approved by its state board of nursing. You need to graduate from a state board approved nursing program in order to be licensed. To find out if the program of your choice is approved, contact its state board of nursing via the information found in Appendix A.

State boards set minimum standards to assure client safety, but many schools go beyond the minimum and obtain national accreditation, which is a voluntary, peer-reviewed, self-regulatory process that demonstrates that their program meets a higher standard. There are two recognized forms of accreditation, institutional and professional. Institutional accreditation focuses on the quality and integrity of the total institution in meeting its own mission, goals, and expected outcomes. Professional accreditation centers on professional programs of study, assessing the extent to which these programs achieve their mission, goals, and expected outcomes and determining the quality of the program and the educational preparation of members of the profession.

Accreditation benefits both the program and the students by:

▶ demonstrating that your nursing program has been evaluated by a qualified, independent group who found it to meet educational purposes in a satisfactory manner.
▶ providing opportunity to licensure and eligibility for entitlement programs.

▶ encouraging the nursing program to participate in ongoing evaluation and to be responsive to areas that need improvement.

▶ assisting employers in seeking graduates who are competent nurses.

▶ offering information for educational and career decision making.

▶ facilitating credit transfer to other institutions.

▶ enabling student eligibility for federal, state, and foundation funding support for programs that don't have regional accreditation.

▶ enabling student eligibility for funding support from federal and state agencies, and foundations for those programs that do not have regional accreditation.

When seeking professional accreditation, most nursing programs utilize either the National League of Nursing Accrediting Commission (NLNAC) or the Commission on Collegiate Nursing Education (CCNE). Both agencies are nationally recognized by the U.S. Department of Education.

National League of Nursing Accrediting Commission (NLNAC)

The NLNAC accredits post-secondary and higher degree nursing programs—practical, diploma, associate degree, baccalaureate degree, master's degree, and clinical doctorate degree programs. It functions on the belief that accreditation contributes to the uniqueness of nursing for the benefit of the public, as well as the enhancement of nursing educational quality with continuous self-assessment, planning, and improvement. Accreditation shows the public and the educational community that the accredited nursing program is working to achieve its educational objectives and is in compliance with established criteria and standards for current and anticipated practice.

Commission on Collegiate Nursing Education (CCNE)

The CCNE serves the public interest by ensuring the quality and integrity of baccalaureate and graduate level nursing educational programs. CCNE accreditation accomplishes five purposes:

1. to hold programs accountable to the community of interest—nursing, consumers, employers, higher education, students, and their families—by assuring that the programs have mission statements,

goals and outcomes appropriate for programs that prepare people to enter the nursing profession

2. to evaluate the program's success in achieving its mission, goals, and outcomes

3. to assess the extent to which the program meets accreditation standards

4. to inform the public about accredited programs and the value and purpose of accreditation

5. to foster ongoing improvement in nursing education programs and thus professional nursing practice.

NURSING NOTES
The Student Experience, by Kelly Peterson

I first thought the large amount of hard work and dedication that I put into my career as a student, the hours that I spent at the library doing NCLEX questions, and the times that I studied for weeks and ended up with a B on a test. (My non-nursing major friends still don't understand why I am unhappy when I receive a B. I guess I really don't either, other than the undying mantra that plays in my head saying "Dean's List or else" that began to sing to me the fall of my freshman year.) I also thought about how jealous I was when my non-nursing major roommates used to come home from "dollar mixed drinks night" at the bar at 3:30 A.M. and wake me up merely one hour before I had to get up for my Saturday maternity clinical rotation. But then, as it goes, there is a positive flip side to every situation. Of course, I was jealous when my roommates were goofing off and hanging out, but when I got home on Saturday afternoon, I would ask them a question that would never fail to make me see the silver lining in the situation. That question was, "So, what did you guys do today?" Their basic response was that they'd hung out, watched television, gone out to lunch, the typical weekend things that I would also be doing myself the next morning. At that moment, I would think back to what I had done throughout that Saturday morning. Maybe that day I'd held an hour-old newborn, or taught a mother and father how to hold their baby while feeding her because they were unsure and uncomfortable about the best way. Or maybe I'd helped with discharge teaching for the family, including the warning signs of possible problems and things they should look out for to ensure the health of their baby. But even if it was just any one of those scenarios, then that meant that I made a difference in someone's life. I helped an uneasy family to become more comfortable with providing the great care that I knew they would for their new baby, or I helped a family learn the early warning signs for any illnesses or reasons why the baby should be seen by a pediatrician, and therefore a major problem for that child was prevented. Yes, nursing school is challenging, and I will not deny that sometimes I wonder why I didn't choose a major that is less stressful and less time-consuming, but then I remember why I started studying this profession in the first place—to make a difference to someone else, every day. My nursing career so far hasn't only helped others, it has taught me that I do want the best grades, the best job after graduation, and the best opportunities for myself. Also I learned that along with making others feel better, I need to pay attention to myself. I have improved the health of others while at the same time improving the health of myself. To me, that makes these four years worth the struggle. The knowledge that I have gained so far also makes me excited to continue to learn new things and anxious to see the ways in which I will improve myself in the future. The knowledge that I have gained, my nursing major friends that have turned into family, and the increase in my drive to succeed are a few of the reasons why, as hard as nursing school has been, I would not trade it for the world.

Practical Nursing Programs

In 2006, there were more than 1,500 state-approved programs in practical nursing. Most practical nursing programs are housed in technical and vocational schools or community and junior colleges, with other programs located in hospitals, colleges, and universities. Students typically attend full-time (about 40 hours per week) for one year. Classroom hours total about 650 hours, while supervised clinical experience time totals to about 850, for a grand total of 1,500 hours of education. Students receive a diploma or certificate upon graduation.

In 2007, the National Association for Practical Nurse Education and Service (NAPNES), Inc.'s Council of Practical Nurse Educators finalized the "Standards of Practice and Educational Competencies of Graduates of Practical/Vocational Nursing Programs." The purpose of this document is to assist educators in developing and implementing LPN educational curricula, to help LPN students understand the competencies expected of them upon graduation, to enable employers to better utilize LPNs, and to help consumers understand the scope of LPN practice. These standards demonstrate the LPNs' expanded role for the twenty-first century.

Practical nursing programs can be beneficial for those who are seeking a quick training program because they need fast entry into the work world. Once working, you can still choose to advance your career by entering an LPN to RN mobility program.

Registered Nursing: Diploma

Diploma programs were the first educational programs for registered nursing preparation; however, the number of diploma programs has steadily declined. The decline is related to nursing efforts to achieve more professional status and control over nursing practice and the resulting move of nursing education into institutions of higher learning. Only about 70 diploma programs remained in 2006 according to the U.S. Department of Labor.

Diploma programs are usually two- or three-year hospital-based programs, although some are affiliated with community or junior colleges. Those affiliated with colleges often offer an associate degree along with the diploma. Other diploma programs require that students complete prerequisite college courses prior to admission. These prerequisites usually include English, Chemistry, Anatomy and Physiology, Microbiology, Human Development, and Nutrition. If you are considering this option, you may want to consider a diploma program that also offers an associate degree.

Registered Nursing: Associate Degree

Associate degree in nursing (ADN) programs take two to three years to complete and are offered at colleges and universities, particularly community and junior colleges. As noted above, some run in conjunction with hospital diploma programs. There are approximately 850 ADN programs in the United States.

The National Organization for Associate Degree Nursing notes that ADN programs continually evolve to reflect local community needs and current emerging healthcare delivery systems.

ADN programs offer an affordable entry into nursing and provide students with opportunities to bridge into a BSN (bachelor's degree in nursing) program. This is an important consideration. Associate degree programs focus more on technical skills than theory and are often used as a stepping-stone to a BSN, allowing AD nurses to continue working while continuing their education, often with tuition reimbursement from their employers.

Registered Nursing: Baccalaureate Degree

Baccalaureate (bachelor's) degree in nursing (BSN) programs are four- to five-year programs that prepare nurses to practice across all healthcare settings. Colleges and universities offer BSN programs, and 709 nursing programs offered degrees at the bachelor's level in 2006. Like other registered nurse programs, BSN options prepare nurses to take the NCLEX-RN, but they also include a broad spectrum of scientific, critical thinking, humanistic, communication, and leadership skills, as well as specific courses on community health nursing not typically included in diploma or associate-degree tracks. BSN programs introduce students to the world of nursing research and evidence-based nursing practice.

The BSN is preferred and frequently required for public health nursing, military nursing, school nursing, case management, overseas nursing, and forensic nursing. The American Association of Colleges of Nursing (AACN) and other nursing organizations recognize the BSN as the minimum educational requirement for professional nursing practice.

NURSING NOTES

Second Time Around, by Krista Lee Kelsey

Throughout my life, my biggest aspiration was to become a nurse. Whenever I was asked what I wanted to be when I grew up, my answer would always simply be, "a nurse" with no hesitation. When I would go to the hospital or even to my doctor, I would be fascinated by the care and comfort the nurses provided. Growing up, my aspirations of becoming a nurse never changed; however, my outlook on the path to this rewarding career did. I have had a hearing loss in both ears since I was just a child and although my dream has always been to become a nurse, I constantly thought that nursing was just a dream that could never be achieved due to my disability. I continued with my schooling, but not along the path I had hoped. I received my bachelor of arts degree in Human Development, thinking that this was the suitable choice for me, as in my mind, I could never become a nurse, which was my ultimate goal in life. One day, I watched my close friend graduate from nursing school, and I became overwhelmed with envy. I started thinking, "Why can't I do this? What's holding me back? There's no written law that says that people with disabilities can't become involved with healthcare." So, my quest began. As soon as I came to this realization, which would ultimately change my life, I began to search on the Internet, trying to find someone with the same story as me. To my surprise, I found numerous hearing impaired nurses sharing their stories, which set the rest of my life in stone. I started calling around to local nursing retailers, asking if they had a certain stethoscope that amplifies the sounds that nurses hear on a daily basis. Although I could not find it locally, I was able to order it online. It was a bit pricey, but definitely worth it. After struggling through my first semester of nursing school due to my hearing loss, I looked into getting accommodations for my disability. I was directed to the Services for Students with Disabilities office, and they provided me with many accommodations. For instance, they have provided a wonderful note-taker for my classes. Services for Students with Disabilities, along with my note-taker and two amazing Instructors, have finally made my lifelong dream come true.

Registered Nursing: Accelerated Second Degree

As noted in Chapter 1, one of the reasons for the graying of nursing is that more "mature" people are entering nursing programs. Nursing has become a very popular second career option, even for people who were seasoned in their previous career, including those with other degrees. In general, second-degree nursing students are older than traditional students. They tend to be highly motivated and goal directed, and they typically express themselves throughout their nursing educational experience regarding their specific needs, the curriculum, and how courses are run. They also tend to be highly regarded by their employers once they begin to practice.

As people search for more rewarding or lucrative careers, an increasing number of universities offer nursing programs for students who already have a bachelor's degree or even a master's or doctoral degree in a field other than Nursing. Accelerated programs and second degree options make it faster, though not easier. These programs date back to 1970; however, they have proliferated in the past 17 years, primarily as a response to the nursing shortage.

According to the American Association of Colleges of Nursing, there were 205 second degree programs in 2008, compared to 91 in 1990. These programs are shorter than traditional programs and are ideal for students who don't want to spend another four years obtaining another undergraduate degree.

Accelerated programs require that students complete prerequisite courses prior to admission. These courses may include Anatomy and Physiology, Chemistry, Microbiology, Nutrition, Human Development, Psychology, and Sociology. Accelerated programs are quite intense and fast-paced; however they allow second-degree students to obtain their BSN in as little as 12 months.

Registered Nursing: Master's Degree Entry

Some universities offer a master's entry program for students with non-nursing degrees. These programs may prepare you to be an advanced practice nurse or a clinical nurse leader. Advanced practice preparation programs are typically three years in length and provide the components of entry-level education to allow students to sit for the NCLEX licensure exam and then move directly into specialty advanced practice courses. Accelerated advance practice programs usually require you to pass the NCLEX prior to completing the final year of your advanced practice courses. Advanced practice options are explored in detail in Chapter 4.

Accelerated programs that lead to graduation as a **clinical nurse leader** (CNL) also tend to have the two-phase process, but instead of advanced practice, students complete second phase coursework that leads to becoming a clinical nurse leader after completion of the first phase entry level courses and taking the NCLEX exam. An emerging master's level role created by the AACN, "The CNL oversees the lateral integration of care for a distinct group of patients and may actively provide direct patient care in complex situations. The CNL puts evidence-based practice into action to ensure that patients benefit from the latest innovations in care delivery. The CNL collects and evaluates patient outcomes, assesses cohort risk, and has the decision-making authority to change care plans when necessary. This clinician functions as part of an interprofessional team by communicating, planning, and implementing care directly with other health care professionals, including physicians, pharmacists, social workers, clinical nurse specialists, and nurse practitioners. The CNL role is not one of administration or management. The CNL is a leader in the health care delivery system in all settings in which health care is delivered, not just the acute care setting. Implementation of this role will vary across settings." CNLs are eligible to sit for a national board certification through the AACN.

CHOOSING THE RIGHT PROGRAM FOR YOU

With a cornucopia of programs to choose from, how do you select the one that's right for you? You definitely want to choose a program that is approved by your state board of nursing so that you can sit for the NCLEX exam and get your license, but that still leaves the field wide open. Answering the following questions may help narrow it down.

1. Which level of nursing is best for me—LPN, RN diploma, RN associate degree, RN baccalaureate degree, RN accelerated program? Consider your background, the time you can devote to your education, and the opportunities you want to pursue for your career. Keep in mind that a baccalaureate degree offers the most opportunity, but that you can obtain your bachelor's degree via a mobility program if you cannot afford to go to school full-time for four years now. Some hospitals offer tuition assistance for nurses who continue their education.

2. Should I attend an accredited nursing program? Remember from Chapter 1 that accreditation from an independent nursing agency differs from state board approval. You should take this into consideration if you plan to continue your nursing education because most advance degree programs require that you graduate from an accredited program to be admitted. Although you may now think you'll never go to school again, never say never—you may change your mind in a few years.

3. How much can I afford? For many people, this is the deciding question. You should consider what you can pay now and how much debt

you want to incur if you take out student loans. College can be expensive, but graduation from a prestigious nursing program can have its merit (not to mention financial aid). Major hospitals do seek out nursing graduates from schools known to turn out excellent nurses, and these facilities tend to pay the premium salaries.

4. How far am I willing to travel? If you are a high school student with wanderlust, you may want a school as far from home as possible, giving you plenty of options. But if you're a single mom, you'll want to be close to home and may want a program that affords you schedule options and/or child care facilities.

5. What is the quality of the nursing faculty? Ask about the faculty. In its August 2008 paper *Nursing Faculty Qualifications and Roles*, the National Council of State Boards of Nursing (NCSBN) recommends that full- and part-time nursing faculty in both practical nursing and registered nursing programs have either a master's degree or doctoral degree in nursing. For LPN programs, other faculty, including those who are BSN-prepared, may participate on a nursing faculty team to enrich and augment nursing education. For RN programs, other supportive faculty with graduate degrees in related fields may participate on a nursing faculty team to enrich and augment nursing education. If you see yourself publishing or performing research, ask if there are faculty members who can mentor you in these processes. University faculty members are often required to "publish or perish," and many participate in faculty-student research programs, which may result in your being published before you graduate. But faculty members in other facilities also write books and articles, or perform nursing research, so don't hesitate to ask about this wherever you consider applying for admission.

6. What facilities does the program offer? Does the program have a state-of-the-art nursing laboratory? Nurses perform a number of clinical skills, and you first learn most of these in the nursing lab. Today's modern labs come fully equipped with more than stethoscopes and bedpans; they have a full range of technological wonders, including equipment for simulated experiences that allow you to practice on computerized mannequins that respond to your assessments and interventions. Programs should also offer a wide range of clinical experiences. All levels

should have adequate hospital experiences, and baccalaureate programs should also have critical care and community experiences. Ask about their partner facilities, questioning the who, what, when, where, and why. Who will precept or supervise you at the facility, and what are their qualifications? What will you be expected to do at the facilities? Make sure you will get adequate hands-on experience. When will you attend the facilities: day or evening; how many hours a day; how many days a week; and how many weeks of the program? Where are the facilities? Are they within walking distance, or will you need transportation to drive several miles away from the nursing program? Why were the facilities chosen? Were they selected because they provide the best experience or solely because of their proximity to the nursing program?

Once you narrow your options, contact the programs and ask if you can spend a day at each one to get the feel of it. Talk to faculty and students and ask them what they think of the program. Sit in on a nursing class to see how they teach and to find out if their classrooms are high-tech. This will also give you an idea of class size; some programs have as few as 20 to 30 students in each class, while others have more than 100. Ask about their non-nursing course requirements, including science and liberal arts. Check out the nursing laboratory and the library. You'll do a lot of reading, so ask about library accessibility, both live and virtual. If you plan to live on campus, check out the dorms. Finally, spend some time at a clinical site. Your options may be limited due to client confidentiality, but you can at least see the facility and learn the faculty-to-student clinical ratio.

NURSING NOTES

Contact: That First Clinical, by Valerie Hermann

I couldn't wait to get my first patient's medical history information to learn what I would be dealing with during my first clinical experience. Although I am not fond of nursing homes and knew it would be a challenge, I was really excited to get to know my resident. However, my excitement turned to excitement plus anxiety when I finally read my resident's long list of health issues. After looking up definitions for the afflictions, I found out that my first patient, among her other ailments, had had a stroke and couldn't speak or swallow well. I was so worried that I wouldn't give this resident the proper care or that I might forget any one of her many diagnoses and put her in danger.

The first day of clinical I was extremely nervous about meeting my resident. All I had to do was introduce myself and get to know her, but I kept thinking of how my next visit was going to be a bed bath with this stranger. After meeting her, however, I felt better being able to put a face with her name. She was the oldest person I'd ever met, but she had a lively spark.

After a month of giving care to my resident I was far more at ease and comfortable around her. I also became more confident in my nursing skills. Due to the lack of verbal communication, I was always unsure whether my resident was physically comfortable or if she needed anything. I had to always be aware of her facial expressions and nonverbal cues, such as hand gestures. Honestly, I never felt confident at the end of my shift that I had done everything she needed or that she even was comfortable around me.

On my last day of clinical, I was bathing and dressing her for the last time. Since my skills were improving, we had extra time to visit before I had to leave. Although she couldn't talk to me, we had a great conversation. She showed me pictures of her children and cards she'd received on her 90th birthday. Right before they wheeled her away I asked if she had enjoyed having me give her care. She nodded and then with all her might, she squeaked out a "Yes." I felt so much better knowing for sure that she had been comfortable with my skills while working with her. I hope she knew how much that one little word meant to me.

MOBILITY PROGRAMS

Those of you who desire a BSN but cannot afford the time or money to attend a four-year college can consider starting at the LPN, diploma, or AD level and entering a mobility program after obtaining your nursing license. Another benefit of choosing this route is that many of these programs are online. *Accredited online programs* offer the same education as accredited brick-and-mortar programs, but are more convenient for many students, especially for those with full-time jobs and/or families. However, you do need to be self-motivated and self-directed with good time management and organizational skills to do well in an online program. If you are interested in an online program, ask them how they handle the clinical practicum courses. Some have residency requirements, while others allow you to complete clinical practicums near where you live.

Is an Online Program for You?

Advantages of Online Programs	Disadvantages of Online Programs
Accessibility: you can attend class from virtually anywhere	Occasional technological problems
Flexibility: you work at your own pace, on your own time	Need to be self-directed
	Limited access to faculty
No or minimal travel expenses	Limited interaction with peers
Diversity of student population	Employers may still view online degree as inferior to brick-and-mortar degree
Most documents are readily available	Some courses may not be offered online

LPN to BSN

LPN to BSN programs allow LPNs to graduate with their BSN in two to three years. These programs provide students with professional foundations and health assessment as well as promotion, pathophysiology, nursing research, informatics, community health, critical care, and leadership. Prerequisites usually include: Introduction to Human Anatomy & Physiology I and II, Psychology, and Chemistry. Some LPN to BSN programs allow LPNs to earn as many as 30 credits by taking advanced placement tests, which validate their previous knowledge. Students sit for the NCLEX-RN upon completion.

RN to BSN

Earning a BSN opens more avenues of opportunities for nurses, especially in specialized practice and management. RN to BSN programs enable RNs to assume roles that demand critical thinking, decision making, and leadership skills. Advanced standing is granted to RNs when they enter

BSN programs, but the nature of this advanced standing is typically individualized based on the RN's previous educational (and sometimes experiential) background. Admission requirements usually include official transcripts from the diploma or associate degree accredited nursing program; all other college transcripts; a GPA of 2.5 or equivalent; high school transcript; letters of reference; and a resume.

RN to MSN

The RN to MSN option (also called "bridge program") is ideal for RNs who have baccalaureate degrees in other disciplines, or RNs who wish to progress rapidly once they obtain their BSN. These programs are highly selective and typically require the RN to successfully complete a certain amount of the BSN before being considered for admission. But the advantage is that you complete your MSN in a shorter period of time.

ADMISSION REQUIREMENTS

Admission requirements vary somewhat for each level program and for each institution. To learn about the requirements for your intended programs, contact their admissions office. All programs require that you submit an admissions application, and most charge a processing fee. Many require a criminal background check prior to admission; most require this before you work with clients. Other programs require a caregiver background check, which reviews any previous professional licenses and credentials, and searches social service records for any history of abuse or neglect. Nursing programs may also require recent letters of reference from people other than relatives and close friends. Students are responsible for assuring that admission requirements are met and that all materials are received by the admissions office prior to the deadline date. However, a completed admissions packet does not guarantee admission to a nursing program. You should also know that most full-time nursing programs advise students against working full-time due to the rigorous nature of the nursing education.

Admission to a practical nursing program generally requires:

▶ a high school transcript or scores from a Certificate of General Education Development (GED) or High School Equivalency Diploma (HSED)

▶ transcripts from any colleges attended

▶ high school GPA (grade point average) of 2.0 or greater

▶ completion of at least two high school math courses with a grade of C or better or completion of a one-semester college math course

▶ completion of at least two high school science courses with a grade of C or better or completion of a one-semester college science course

▶ satisfactory score on an admission assessment test such as the SAT, ASSET, ACT, or COMPASS (essentially, these test your verbal, reading, and numerical skills)

Admission to an associate degree (AD) registered nursing program typically requires:

▶ a high school transcript or scores from a Certificate of General Education Development (GED) or High School Equivalency Diploma (HSED)

▶ transcripts from any colleges attended

▶ high school GPA (grade point average) of 2.5 or greater

▶ grade of C or better in algebra, biology, and chemistry, or equivalents (college courses taken within the last five to seven years and passed with a grade of C or better; acceptable score on National League for Nurses [NLN] preadmission exam)

Admission requirements for RN diploma programs may be similar to either the LN requirements or AD requirements, depending on the program.

Admission to a baccalaureate nursing (BSN) registered nursing program typically requires:

▶ a high school transcript or scores from a Certificate of General Education Development (GED) or High School Equivalency Diploma (HSED)

▶ transcripts from any colleges attended

▶ high school GPA (grade point average) of 2.75 or greater

▶ completion of four years of high school English; three years of mathematics that includes algebra and geometry; three years of science that includes biology and chemistry (some also require physics); three years of social studies; and two years of the same foreign language.

▶ some BSN nursing programs have a two-part admission process, whereby the student is first accepted into the college/university and then the nursing program (admission to the college/university does not guarantee admission into the nursing program in many of these schools)

▶ some BSN nursing programs begin their nursing courses in the junior year and require that a specific number of college credits be completed prior to the student being admitted into the nursing program

Admission requirements to accelerated second-degree programs typically include:

▶ completion of baccalaureate or higher degree from an accredited university

▶ official transcripts from all colleges and/or universities attended

▶ minimum cumulative GPA of 3.0 from all colleges and/or universities attended

▶ an essay on why you want to be a nurse

▶ three recent letters of reference from people other than relatives or close friends

▶ a face-to-face or telephone interview with the program director or admissions committee

▶ TOEFL score of 550 (paper-based), 213 (computer-based), or 79 (new Internet-based) for English as a Second Language (ESL) students

▶ Accelerated second-degree applicants must complete the following prerequisites:
  Human Anatomy & Physiology I and II (4 credits each)
  Microbiology (4 credits)
  Chemistry (4 credits)
  Introduction to Psychology

Introduction to Sociology, Humanities, and Social Sciences (at least 10 credits)

Statistics

Electives

Some nursing programs have additional requirements that must be met between acceptance into and initiation of the program. These include:

▶ special fees to hold the student's assigned clinical seat
▶ completed health and immunization forms
▶ evidence of current cardiopulmonary resuscitation (CPR) certification with either the Red Cross Basic Life Support (BLS) or the American Heart Association BLS for the Healthcare Provider.
▶ verification of current state-tested nursing assistant certification

Given the competitive and rigorous nature of all nursing programs, be prepared. If you are a high school student, work with your advisor to assure that you have the required coursework and GPA, and prep for your preadmission test(s). If you are an adult student, work with the nursing program advisor to assure that you can meet all the admission requirements. All applicants should consider volunteering at a local hospital and brushing up on computer skills.

TUITION AND OTHER COSTS

Post-secondary education costs have soared in recent years. Some programs are less expensive than others, but many of the larger, more expensive schools have more opportunities for financial aid, which may make their cost comparable to or even less expensive than smaller schools. Regardless of where you attend nursing school, tuition is only part of the cost. Additional costs include room and board, transportation, books and other supplies, and laboratory fees.

FINANCIAL AID

Given the cost of education, most people can benefit from financial aid, and there are many grants, loans, scholarships, and loan forgiveness programs available to hard-working students.

Online, you can find numerous resources for college preparation, including planning for and obtaining financial aid, which has been modified here with a nursing touch.

High school juniors should look into: tuition costs; admission, and financial aid application deadlines; state, federal, and school aid programs based on both need and merit; unique aid opportunities (community service awards, children of veterans awards, first-generation college student awards, etc.); and the annual cost increase of college expenses. Fall is the time to take the PSAT, attend financial aid nights, and start looking for scholarships. In winter, prep for the SAT or ACT and build a portfolio (awards, report cards, honors, evidence of hospital volunteer activities, newspaper clippings—whatever sets you apart from other students). Come spring, talk to the college financial aid counselor and ask for an early estimate, and take the SAT or ACT. When summer rolls around, get to work, literally. Make money and put it aside for your nursing program incidentals.

High school seniors should check out: the graduation debt burden at each of their potential nursing programs; how long it takes to graduate and whether the financial aid will be similar each year; availability of financial aid for study abroad. They and their parent(s) should also obtain a personal identification number (PIN) for Free Application for Federal Student Aid (FAFSA) processing. In the fall, compare and contrast nursing program requirements for application materials and financial aid forms. Some only require the FAFSA; others the PROFILE, a form administered by the College Scholarship Service (CSS), the financial division of the College Board. Many private colleges and universities require the CSS PROFILE to determine your eligibility for non-government financial aid, including the institution's own aid. Remember to be attentive to all application deadlines, retake the SAT or ACT if you're not satisfied with your scores, and spend some more time at financial aid nights. Warm up the winter by filing your FAFSA online; this is your gateway to aid at schools nationwide. Proof and correct your Student Aid Report (SAR) and organize your financial aid award letters to ease the job of comparing and contrasting colleges. Come spring, assess your situation; if you didn't get aid at your school of choice, visit and appeal to them in person. They may take a second look. Make your decision; May 1 is the deadline for final decisions at most schools.

Grants

Grants are free money; you don't have to pay them back. Money is dwindling in today's economy, but there are still thousands of grant programs in the United States, many specifically targeted to nursing. Schools often automatically consider you for grants when you complete your FAFSA; however, some grants require that you submit a proposal. Applying for these grants takes time and effort, but it's worth it, even for grants that pay $1,000 or less.

Scholarships

Scholarships typically recognize academic achievement, athletic ability, or artistic accomplishments. They are competitive, but, like grants, do not need to be paid back. Some have restrictions and may apply only to students in a specific type of nursing program or to nursing students who belong to a specific organization or group. Most require that you have and maintain a high GPA and demonstrate professional behavior, which means you don't want to have anything embarrassing on your Facebook or MySpace page. Nursing specialty societies offer scholarships, but usually on the graduate level. The best sources for other nursing students are religious organizations, private and public schools, small businesses, corporations, community groups, generous individuals, or philanthropic foundations.

The U.S. Department of Health and Human Services Health Resources and Services Administration (HRSA) offers nursing scholarships. In exchange for at least two years of service in a critical nursing shortage area, the Nursing Scholarship Program pays tuition, required fees, other reasonable costs (required books, clinical supplies, laboratory expenses, etc.), and a monthly stipend. For information and an application, go to http://bhpr.hrsa.gov/nursing/scholarship.

Student Loans and Loan Forgiveness

Student loans require payback, but at a low interest rate with payments due starting six months after graduation, or sooner if you decrease your credit load to less than half-time. The nursing shortage has cased the burden of student loans with a growing number of loan forgiveness programs. These programs offer to pay back or forgive student loan debt in exchange for service. Typically, one year of the loan is forgiven for each year that the nurse serves in an area of need after graduation. You gain experience while you lose payments.

The U.S. Department of Health and Human Services Health Resources and Services Administration (HRSA) offers the Nursing Education Loan Repayment Program (NELRP), which is a competitive program that repays 60% of the qualifying loan balance of registered nurses selected for funding in exchange for two years of service at a critical shortage facility. Participants may also be eligible to work a third year to receive payment of an additional 25% of the qualifying loan balance. This HRSA program requires an application, but certainly is worth the effort. More information is available at http://bhpr.hrsa.gov/nursing/loanrepay.htm.

NURSING NOTES

ROTC, by Katrina Kruczo

I am currently in the ROTC program and upon completion of school will be a 2LT in the United States Army, practicing as an army nurse. Nursing school has been exceptionally challenging for me since I had to balance working part-time, being a cadet, and the heavy workload that nursing entails. At times I found myself just getting by with the grades I needed and lost much sleep studying and preparing for both class and clinical. Even though it is difficult, I know that I have wanted to be a nurse since the second grade and that the trials and tribulations just make me stronger and more determined. It is also rewarding when you have clinical and are able to improve the life of the patients you care for and to me that is what makes the hard work worth it.

RESERVE OFFICERS TRAINING CORPS

The Reserve Officers Training Corps (ROTC) is a training program that prepares college students to become commissioned officers. This is a unique opportunity that provides additional clinical experiences for nursing students and offers them financial assistance for their education. It also provides you with tools and support that help you manage the difficulties of the nursing curriculum.

Army ROTC

The Army ROTC is an elective curriculum taken with your required college classes. You will have a normal college student experience like other students, but when you graduate you will be an officer in the U.S. Army. The Army ROTC Nurse Program offers valuable leadership experience and training that can benefit you in either a military or private sector nursing career. Nurse cadets can paticipate in a paid, three-week Nurse Summer Training Program and be assigned to army hospitals throughout the United States and Germany. This program introduces you to the Army Medical Department and to the roles and responsibilities of an Army Nurse Corps officer. You receive one-on-one, hands-on experience while under the supervision of an experienced Army Nurse Corps officer. This opportunity allows you to fine-tune your nursing skills, develop problem-solving techniques and become comfortable with developing your professional skills as a member of the U.S. Army Healthcare Team. The Army ROTC Nurse Program offers two-, three-, or four-year scholarships that pay tuition, books, fees, and living allowances. For more information on the Army ROTC go to www.goarmy.com/rotc/index.jsp.

Air Force ROTC

The Air Force ROTC prepares you to become an Air Force officer with a career that carries a high level of responsibility, accountability, and professionalism. They say that if you can make it in the Air Force, you can make it anywhere. Air Force ROTC awards Type 2 scholarships (tuition capped at $15,000 per year, plus $900 per year for books). The program is noncompetitive, meaning that those who meet the criteria are awarded a scholarship. Their criteria are that you:

- ▶ are a U.S. citizen
- ▶ pass the Air Force Officer Qualifying Test or have your failing scores waived after two failures

▶ pass the Air Force ROTC Physical Fitness Test

▶ have a 2.5 minimum cumulative GPA

▶ have a complete physical examination as well as certification as commission-qualified by the Department of Defense Medical Examination Review Board

▶ not already be a contracted scholarship recipient

▶ meet the age, moral, and other scholarship eligibility requirements for the Air Force ROTC

▶ be a sophomore or junior nursing major at a National League for Nursing or Commission on Collegiate Nursing Education accredited college or university

Nursing scholarship cadets agree to accept a commission in the Air Force Nurse Corps and serve four years on active duty after successfully completing their licensure exam. For more information about the Air Force ROTC go to www.afrotc.com.

Navy ROTC

The Navy ROTC (NROTC) Nurse Program allows you to practice with the most respected medical professionals in the world and in the most advanced medical centers in the country, and to experience hands-on clinical training that leads more rapidly to managerial positions. Four-year NROTC scholarships are available to students pursuing a Bachelor of Science degree in Nursing (BSN). Upon graduation, NROTC program midshipmen will be commissioned as officers in the Navy Nurse Corps. The NROTC Program lets you focus on your studies and enjoy college life without worrying about how you're going to pay for it all. NROTC students are expected to wear the NROTC uniform once a week, participate in drills with the unit at least once a week, and take a Naval Science course each semester. A NROTC scholarship covers full tuition, all college educational fees, allowance for textbooks, monthly living expense allowance, and other related expenses. Upon graduation, you'll launch your career as an officer in the Navy, receiving a solid salary, comprehensive medical and dental coverage, and 30 days paid vacation each year. The obligation period is four or five years. For more information on NROTC, go to www.navy.com/careers/nrotc.

WORK-STUDY PROGRAMS

Work-study programs assist financial needs by allowing students to work in on-campus jobs, community-related jobs, or assisting teachers. These jobs typically depend on factors such as level of financial need and school funding availability. Students often choose work-study programs that are related to their field of study, which not only helps them finance their education, but also gives them resume experience. Nursing work-study students may assist in the campus laboratory, help with secretarial work, or assist faculty with their service or scholarship load. Work-study pays at least the federal minimum wage, depending on the skills and level of experience needed. If you wish to be considered for work-study assistance, indicate this when completing your FAFSA form.

NURSING CURRICULUM ESSENTIALS

All programs adhere to the essential components of a nursing curriculum so that their students pass the NCLEX exam. However, the NCLEX exam determines entry-level nursing competency; therefore. most programs teach content that reaches beyond the scope of NCLEX to prepare students for their nursing careers. Curriculums vary by level; associate degree nurses typically complete between 60 and 90 credits, while baccalaureate students complete 120 to 150. Hospital or vocational school-based diploma and practical nursing programs use hour-based requirements instead of credits, but still provide content suitable for NCLEX. These programs may also integrate content instead of presenting it as stand-alone courses; for example, they may include pharmacology throughout their nursing courses rather than as a separate pharmacology course.

Several courses are required of all nurses, although their content and intensity may vary by level. Other nursing courses tend to be more specific to baccalaureate programs. Baccalaureate programs also typically allow for elective courses, which can be utilized for career-enhancing minors or concentrations such as Health Administration, Forensics, Psychology, and Gerontology. As you will note by the course descriptions that follow, nursing courses build on each other to provide students with the essentials of client care.

Nursing Fundamentals I & II

As its title signifies, Nursing Fundamentals lays the foundation for the other nursing courses, and your career. The first course includes: an introduction to nursing; theoretical principles such as Maslow's hierarchy of needs and nursing theory; the healthcare delivery system; the roles of the nurse; critical thinking; the nursing process; therapeutic communication; client safety and comfort; and an introduction to disease transmission, infection control, and standard precautions. The second course introduces students to basic nursing skills: therapeutic communication, hand hygiene, making an occupied bed, bed baths, oral care, medication administration, intravenous therapy, wound care, musculoskeletal devices (casts, traction), and blood glucose monitoring. Many programs introduce students to clinical practice in this course, beginning with the nursing skills laboratory and progressing to an acute or long-term care facility. Vital sign assessment—temperature, blood pressure, pulse, and respiration—may be a component of this course or the health assessment course.

Human Anatomy and Physiology I & II

Anatomy is the study of the body's internal and external structures, such as the skin, skeleton, heart, and liver. Physiology is the study of how organs perform their vital functions including digestion and respiration. Human Anatomy and Physiology (A&P) requires two courses to cover its extensive content, and each course consists of lecture and laboratory. The first course begins with A&P at the cellular, chemical, and tissue levels, then moves into the system level, which continues into the second course. Students will study the following systems: integumentary system (skin, hair, and nails), nervous, endocrine, respiratory, lymphatic, immune, cardiac, digestive, urinary, musculoskeletal, and reproductive. You will also learn about fluids and electrolytes, acid-base balance, metabolism, and genetics. A&P creates the foundation for health assessment, pathophysiology, pharmacology, and a large portion of the nursing process. Be advised that dissection of preserved mammalian specimens is required during laboratory sessions.

Microbiology

Microbiology introduces nursing students to the principles and clinical relevance of immunology (how humans fight disease), bacteriology (bacterial diseases), mycology (fungal diseases), virology (viral diseases), and in some cases, parasitology (parasitic diseases). The course includes many etiological agents responsible for global infectious diseases, as well as those that may be utilized as biological weapons. Knowledge about infectious diseases and immune response expands rapidly, thus content may vary when you take the course. Like A&P, microbiology consists of both lecture and laboratory.

Chemistry

Chemistry infiltrates everyday life since things as simple as cooking and cleaning involve chemicals. Our bodies consist of chemicals; chemicals keep us alive (oxygen); and chemicals cause illness (pollution). Nurses use chemicals daily when they administer medications. Nurses take one or two chemistry courses that focus on topics relevant to nursing, such as acids, bases, salts, amino acids, sugars, molality, DNA, and enzymes.

Nutrition

Based on chemistry, the nutrition course offers an introduction to the interrelationship among nutrition, food, and the environment as they impact health. Nutrition focuses on the concepts of nutrition, including chemistry, digestion, absorption, and metabolism of nutrients, as well as the role of diet in chronic illness across the lifespan.

Health Assessment

Health Assessment enables students to develop basic assessment techniques. Students essentially learn how to perform comprehensive subjective and objective data assessment. The course typically begins with interviewing skills, then progresses to the collection of client historical data, and then to system by system physical assessment. Students learn how to inspect, percuss, palpate, and auscultate, using their senses and medical equipment. Students practice interviewing skills and system assessment in the clinical laboratory, and complete the course by performing a head-to-toe physical assessment.

Pharmacology

Pharmacology emphasizes pharmaceutic, pharmokinetic, and pharmacodynamic phases, essentially providing students with detail on why and how medications work. Students learn about specific drug classifications: anti-infective, analgesic, cardiovascular, central nervous system, autonomic nervous system, respiratory tract, gastrointestinal tract, hormones, drugs for fluid and electrolyte balance, hematologic, psychiatric, antineoplastic, immunomodulators, ophthalmic, otic, nasal, topical, nutritional, and complementary alternative medicine. Students also learn pediatric and geriatric considerations, as well as drug interactions.

Adult Health

Adult health spans the curriculum since it encompasses the majority of adult illness, disorders, and traumas faced by nurses. Students learn principles of acute and chronic illness, homeostatis and adaptation, sociocultural factors, fluid and electrolyte imbalance, pain management, perioperative nursing, grieving and bereavement, and end-of-life care. They also develop new skills such as the insertion of nasogastric tubes, tube feedings, oxygen therapy, and tracheotomy care. The course includes lecture, nursing laboratory, and clinical practicum components that cover a myriad of disorders.

Typical Adult Medical/Surgical Problems

System	Disorders
Respiratory	upper airway infections and obstructions; laryngeal cancer; atelectasis; pneumonia; pulmonary edema; pulmonary embolism; asthma; chronic obstructive pulmonary disease; occupational lung diseases; lung cancer; chest trauma
Cardiovascular	dysrhythmias; coronary artery disease; hypertension; myocardial infarction; valvular disorders; cardiomyopathy; heart infections; heart failure
Peripheral vascular	arteriosclerosis; atherosclerosis; aneurysm; thrombosis; thrombophlebitis; lymphatic disorders
Hematologic	anemias; polycythemia; leukemia; lymphoma; bleeding disorders
Gastrointestinal	disorders, infections and cancers of the mouth and neck; cancer of the esophagus, pancreas, stomach, and colorectal area; malabsorption; ulcer disease; gastritis; appendicitis; inflammatory bowel disease
Metabolic and endocrine	hepatitis; gall bladder disease; pancreatitis; diabetes mellitus; disorders of the pituitary, thyroid, parathyroid and adrenal glands
Renal and urinary	glomerulonephritis; nephrosis; acute and chronic renal failure; dialysis; renal cancer; renal trauma; urinary tract infections
Reproductive	erectile dysfunction; benign prostate hypertrophy; prostate cancer; testicular cancer; vasectomy (sexually transmitted diseases and female reproductive problems are usually covered in the women's health course)

Women's Health (Obstetrical and Gynecological Nursing; Maternity Nursing; Childbearing Nursing)

This is the course where you get to see, and assist with, one of the greatest miracles of life—the birth of a baby! Originally this course centered on pregnancy and delivery. These concepts still form the core of women's health, but the content now provides students with other pertinent women's health issues. The primary focus now lies on the physiological and psychological adaptation to functional and dysfunctional health patterns in the child-bearing family. The course addresses the norms, pathophysiology, and nursing care related to pregnancy and childbirth, as well as issues of sexual-reproductive health and gynecological problems over the lifespan. Students learn about pregnancy, fetal development, the stages of the birthing process, newborn care, and the common complications that can arise during these events, such as maternal diabetes, eclampsia, fetal distress, prematurity, and complicated births such as caesarean sections. Students study menopause, fertility problems, sexual dysfunction, sexually transmitted diseases, breast cancer, and gynecological cancers. Some programs include content on high-risk newborns. The course consists of lecture, laboratory, and clinical practicum. Students learn prenatal assessment and teaching, labor and delivery, postpartum assessment, and newborn assessment and care. Students spend their practicum time on the maternity unit, in labor and delivery, in the newborn nursery, in the newborn intensive care unit (if available), and in prenatal clinics. Students may also work in the community providing education, including healthy prenatal nutrition, to pregnant adolescents.

Child and Adolescent Health Nursing (Pediatric Nursing)

For those of you wanting to work with children, here is your course. Pediatrics focuses on the unique developmental and healthcare needs of infants, children, and adolescents (henceforth referred to as children). Course content focuses on the physiological and psychological differences of children, wellness promotion, children's reaction to illness and hospitalization, and pediatric illnesses, such as childhood cancer, cystic fibrosis, asthma, hemophilia, sickle cell anemia, celiac disease, and cerebral palsy. Students learn how to identify, report, manage, and prevent child abuse and neglect, how to work with children with psychiatric problems, how to administer medications and procedures to children, and pediatric health promotion. The course consists of lecture, clinical laboratory, and clinical practicum. While students spend part of their clinical rotation in an acute pediatric hospital setting, much of today's pediatrics is outpatient. Thus, students also work in doctors' offices and clinics, immunization programs, juvenile detention centers, schools, child and adolescent psychiatric settings, home care, and community agencies.

Psychiatric and Mental Health Nursing

Nurses manage psychological issues and psychiatric disorders on a daily basis, regardless of where they work. This course provides the knowledge and experience to work with some of the most severely ill psychiatric clients, enabling you to choose a career as a psychiatric nurse or just apply psychiatric principles wherever you work. The course expands on your knowledge of therapeutic communications and psychiatric medications, and then focuses on the more common psychiatric disorders: major depression, bipolar disorder, the anxiety disorders (obsessive-compulsive disorder, phobias, panic), schizophrenia, eating disorders, personality disorders, substance abuse, domestic violence, Students also learn about various psychiatric therapies: individual, group, and family therapies; art and music therapy; and behavioral therapy. As with other nursing courses, faculty present content in lecture, the nursing laboratory, and clinical settings, such as psychiatric units of general hospitals, state and private psychiatric hospitals, psychiatric clinics, and homeless shelters.

NURSING NOTES

Surviving Junior Year, by Katie Cannizzo

There are two different types of students. There are college students and there are nursing students. Now, in a crowd it is impossible to tell the difference between the two. But hang out in a room with 40 nursing students and after about three minutes you will know 75 different nursing diagnoses specific to you. You will soon realize that the happiness and kindness in the room with nurses is contagious. This is normal;

we are contagious, and nurses show signs of happiness related to the kind-natured people they are as evidenced by laughing and smiling that is uncontrolled.

In nursing, junior year is probably the most challenging of them all. When clinical starts and the professors start teaching out of the classroom and in a real hospital setting, it can get a little scary. Not only did I feel as if it were hectic being in the hospital, but also keeping up with studying for other classes was very difficult for me. In the hospital junior year, it is hard to believe the things that we as students are actually allowed to do. Administering medication, especially medications that require syringes, is scary the first time. I always remind myself that if the professor did not think we were able to do something, then they would not let us do that particular thing. If they did not think we were ready to be in the hospital with real patients, they would not let us be there.

Being a nursing student means having stable relationships with people who believe in you, people who can cheer you on. I have a hard time talking about school to some people. I feel like they do not understand the daily challenges. They do not know what it is like to be learning how to keep another human being alive. Life is such a valuable thing and sometimes people do not think of it that way. There were many times where I felt like quitting. I felt like switching majors. Every other major seemed easier than mine, and all my friends seemed to have so much free time. After a while I came to realize that this major is just a balancing act. There is a delicate balance between school, friendships, and family. There also must be time for fun and relaxing. Although it is very hard to find this balance (for me it took two years), the most challenging part is maintaining it once the balance is found.

It feels so good to be able to say that I am studying to be a nurse. I talk to the nurses in the hospital at clinical. Some of them enjoy the conversation and some act as if they cannot be bothered. I also speak a lot with my professors. This really helps with the whole experience, especially when they have life experiences to share. My professors are so knowledgeable; they are people to look up to, to aspire to be. I am a student, lucky to be receiving an education. I am a nursing student and someday with all this hard work, I hope somebody will look up to me. What I sometimes forget, however, is that people already look up to student nurses. They have kind hearts, a gentle touch, and more love than one can ever imagine. I am rewarded every day in some way—and being a nurse, these rewards will be constant throughout my career. This is important to remember, this is something to strive for, this will be my life and I am proud of it.

The following courses are more common in BSN programs:

Community Health Nursing: All nursing courses encompass some form of community nursing, but with the student focusing on individuals. This course focuses on working with whole communities and groups, using principles of public health, epidemiology, environmental health, and case management. Students learn and experience school nursing, occupational nursing, rehabilitation nursing, disaster nursing, correctional health nursing, parish nursing, rural nursing, and home care. This course gives students added independence to synthesize previous nursing knowledge with community health principles. Practicums occur practically anywhere, including health departments, housing complexes, and shopping malls.

Critical Care Nursing: If you love hands-on skills and advanced critical thinking, you'll love this course. Critical care nursing provides the basic principles for working with very ill clients in intensive care and emergency units, as well as in acute and home care, since sicker clients are living longer. Nurses learn the use and analysis of complex monitoring systems, and the assessment and management of complex, life-threatening illnesses.

Nursing Research: This course provides an introduction to and application of the principles and process of research in professional nursing practice. Content includes principles of evidence-based practice, study of research design, data collection techniques, interpretation and critique of nursing research, literature and reports, and the development of the ability to become a discriminating consumer of nursing research. Some programs encourage students to create an evidence-based practice project, while others require a small research project.

Nursing Leadership: Nursing Leadership focuses on the nurse's role as caregiver, advocate, teacher, and leader/manager in promoting, restoring, and maintaining adaptive responses in individuals experiencing complex health problems. Students continue to use the nursing process, while they develop case management skills in collaboration with the interdisciplinary health team. The clinical practicum portion of this course gives students an opportunity to utilize leadership and management skills at the hospital unit level.

Professional Issues in Nursing: This course varies from one institution to another and may include the health care system, the health care crisis, the nursing shortage, ethical issues in nursing, legal issues including malpractice, and global health. The course is strictly didactic and typically presented in a discussion seminar format.

Nursing Electives: Nursing electives provide students with the opportunity to immerse themselves in a nursing specialty area and learn about nursing practice from a variety of different perspectives. Electives vary per program but include: informatics, genetics, gerontology, forensics, rural nursing, emergency nursing, study abroad, human sexuality, end-of-life care, risk management, disaster preparedness, spiritual care, parish nursing, nursing history, cancer nursing, HIV/AIDS, transcultural nursing, and holistic nursing. Chapter 6 contains descriptions of many of these nursing specialties.

NURSING EXTERNSHIPS

Nursing externships increase students' competence and clinical competency. Students work under the direct supervision of a registered nurse, observing and participating in a variety of clinical experiences, often in the clinical specialty of the student's choice. Externships typically take place over the summer, usually between junior and senior year in BSN programs, unrelated to the student's nursing program, and at a facility of the student's choice.

Externships provide several advantages. Most run on 12-hour shifts, offer individualized orientation programs and ongoing educational offerings, and allow students to experience the nursing specialty they hope to practice. Externships pay competitive salaries, providing students with income to use for college costs, save for the future, or use for fun money, and they create a comfort zone that minimizes the reality shock that often occurs when going from student to nurse. Most importantly, externships are career builders. Students frequently obtain preferred employment at their place of externship. Those who choose to work elsewhere have the advantage of enhanced experience, increasing their chances of getting the job they want.

Externships are very competitive. They require that students have completed most of their nursing courses with a strong GPA. Students must submit an application, as well as an essay, resume, transcript, and letters of reference from two or three of their nursing faculty. If you're interested in an externship, start looking well before you plan to begin. Contact your hospitals of interest and ask what they have to offer. Talk to your instructors, as they often know what externships are available, and get your application packet ready by early spring of your junior year.

SERVICE LEARNING

Service learning unites community service with learning objectives to create an activity that will change both the recipient and the provider of the service. Some nursing programs mandate that nursing students complete 10 to 20 hours of service learning each year. These hours are in addition to your clinical practicum hours, but still constitute part of your coursework because the service activities connect to course objectives. Students usually write journals or logs describing their experiences, goal attainment, and feelings, and they share this information with the class.

While service learning may just seem like busy work or forced volunteering, it has considerable advantages. The most important two are gaining resume experience and enriching your life. Experiences include working in soup kitchens, day care centers, prisons, and long-term care. Some students work with established organizations like the Red Cross or Habitat for Humanity, while others save their hours to work during spring break in a needy country or part of the United States. No matter where you serve, you learn something related to nursing, such as assessing for health risk factors or learning how to care for profoundly disabled children.

NURSING NOTES

You Can Do It! by Paige Reynolds

As I begin my last semester of my fourth and final year as a nursing student, I look back and truly have no regrets regarding my career choice. From the beginning I knew nursing was what I wanted, and I wasn't going to let anyone or anything stand in my way. Throughout my first year of college I remained on a waiting list for the nursing program. I worked diligently with determination to do well in my classes and prove that I deserved to be in the nursing program. At the end of my first year I was told that, because of my SAT scores, there was no way I would be admitted to the nursing program. At that point I was willing to leave my first-choice school and continue my career in nursing elsewhere. During the second week of summer I received an e-mail congratulating me on my acceptance into the nursing program. I was ecstatic! I will never forget that day—rereading that e-mail two times over before calling my parents with the amazing news. My hard work and drive to succeed finally paid off.

From that point on, I knew college was going to become more challenging, and I was ready to take it head-on. Throughout my following years as a nursing major I learned more than I ever thought I could, and the best part was that I enjoyed doing it. The major demanded hours upon hours of studying and hard work and as junior year came to an end I was struggling quite a bit. I was determined to get past the finals and continue on to my senior year, and so I did. I knew I needed help with reading and made sure I sought out the right people and received the help that I needed. After reading specialist and psychologist appointments, I finally understood why I was struggling. At the age of 21 and about to enter my senior year of college, I was diagnosed with attention deficit hyperactive disorder (ADHD). I was told that my whole life I had compensated for this and I finally hit a point where it was all too much to take on myself.

Since then I have done my absolute best in academics and couldn't be happier. Becoming a nurse has had its rewarding highs and its lowest of lows, and I wouldn't trade it for the world. I believe nursing is one of the most rewarding careers, which is why I love what I do. In nursing it's the little things that can change a patient's view on life, or even just for that day, and it's an amazing feeling to be able to do that. I have had a good number of patients tell me that just by the care that I give them and my mannerisms they can tell that I will go far in my career and become a wonderful nurse. You will never know the satisfaction of just those few words coming from a stranger, until you experience it yourself.

All in all I leave you with a few words of advice. Never let anyone or anything get in your way or tell you you're not smart enough to become a nurse. If it's what you want, then go for it, and don't stop until you're there. Don't be afraid to seek help, because everyone can use it from time to time. Remember, the books, readings, and tests are just one part of nursing. The other half I believe is the most important, the care of patients. If you have the work ethic and determination to succeed, then you will. Just remember to keep your heart in it as well, because without that, you won't get the rewarding satisfaction of touching the hearts of millions of lives throughout your career.

CHAPTER four

ADVANCED NURSING EDUCATION

GRADUATE EDUCATION (master's and doctoral degrees) enables nurses to assume advanced roles in education, administration, research, and clinical practice. Advanced clinical practice nurses are nurse practitioners, clinical nurse specialists, nurse midwives, and nurse anesthetists. Nurses with graduate education bring new ideas and insights to nursing and the entire healthcare system, and they often influence the political system to effect change. Some of these roles developed because of change. Advanced practice nurses first evolved because of a shortage of physicians, then proliferated in response to managed care. Opportunities for nurses to redefine the role and practice of nursing continue to arise in these times when people demand change.

MASTER'S LEVEL NURSING EDUCATION

The number of master's level programs for advanced practice nursing increased dramatically in the 1990s and early twenty-first century. Most of the increase was in nurse practitioner programs in response to the demand for cost-effective care. However, schools continued to offer graduate degrees in nursing administration and education. Regardless of the role offered, the American Association of Colleges of Nursing (AACN) recommends that all master's level curricula share the same core content:

- ▶ critical thinking and clinical judgment
- ▶ primary healthcare, health promotion, patient education, self-care, rehabilitation, and alternative healthcare
- ▶ practice in multiple settings, including nontraditional settings (prisons, homeless shelters)
- ▶ outcome measures, quality indicators, case management, research methods, healthcare policy and economics, financial management, legislative advocacy, and management of data and technology

Master's curricula vary according to role and specialty; however, core content tends to be consistent in each program. Recommendations are that all master's programs have a core foundation curriculum that addresses theoretical foundations of nursing practice; research; policy, organization, and financing of healthcare; ethics; professional role development; human diversity and social issues; and health promotion and disease prevention. As with undergraduate programs, the content may be integrated into multiple courses or exist in stand-alone courses as in the following course examples.

Issues in Advanced Nursing

This course provides students with the opportunity to analyze contemporary issues and trends as they relate to advanced nursing, including professional role development, legal issues, healthcare policy, cultural diversity, and alternative healthcare practices.

Nursing Ethics

This course explores ethical principles in U.S. healthcare and nursing. It utilizes the American Nurses Association's *Code of Ethics for Nurses* as a framework and familiarizes students in the healthcare decision making involving ethical principles.

Nursing Research I & II

Research I & II present the concepts and process of research, including problem formulation, rights of human subjects, research design, sampling, instrument evaluation, and data collection and analysis strategies. The courses provide students with the opportunity to analyze and critique various quantitative and qualitative nursing research studies, including their implications for utilization, and they emphasize the integration of theoretical and methodological elements in the development of research proposals. Finally, the courses examine research utilization, evidence-based practice, and the application of statistics.

While most advanced practice nurses now hold master's degrees, future advanced practice nurses and nurse administrators will most likely need to obtain a doctoral degree. The new requirement for these roles will be the Doctor of Nursing Practice, while the standard for the nurse educator will remain either master's level or doctoral level (PhD), depending on the nurse's educational role.

NURSING NOTES

From AD to Geriatric NP, by Kathryn Ericksen

Becoming a geriatric nurse evolved over many years in my career as an RN. I first graduated 16 years ago with an associate's degree in nursing. I then ventured to hospital care floor nursing. It proved to be a great challenge with many rewards. The same story that you hear now applied back then as well, "short-staffed, overworked, underpaid." This is when I discovered that being a nurse came from my heart and soul. I wasn't in it for the money; I was in it for the love of it. The satisfaction I felt from helping others and witnessing most of them feeling better and going home was ultimately rewarding.

From hospital nursing I decided to slow the pace a bit and work at a nursing home. Well, the pace wasn't any slower, but the reward was even bigger for me. Still overworked, underpaid, and short-staffed, I was in my element. I had finally landed where I knew I wanted to grow into the role of a geriatric nurse. The passion of working with the geriatric population developed after having worked so closely with them. It helped me to develop emotionally and spiritually as well as clinically. Every day I left the nursing home with a better sense of being. I had developed true heartfelt warmth for the residents.

The residents in the nursing home opened my eyes to a whole new way of thinking about life. It is difficult to put into words, but the epiphany is profound. While working in the nursing home, I realized that most of the residents were not going back to their own homes. This was it, their last residence before they died. So, I tried even harder to make their stays meaningful and dignified. The geriatric patients also offered me so much in return—including their wisdom, strength, spirit, and generosity in sharing of life events.

The elderly population is growing exponentially. With this, I've also learned that geriatric patients are challenging in many ways regarding the chronicity and complexities of their diseases. There are many differences between adults and older adults with the same disease. Treatment and management proves to be much more complex and fragile. The physiological changes, their coexisting comorbidities, and multiple medications place them at a higher risk for complications. As a result of this realization, I felt being an RN on the floor was no longer enough for me. I wanted to contribute more to helping elders in their final weeks to years of life while delivering a high quality of care.

So, with the challenge of deciding to learn more about clinical decision making, holistic care, and prevention strategies (with the best interest of the geriatric patient in mind), I went back to school and succeeded in obtaining my bachelor's degree and have progressed to the master's GNP program. I will graduate with my master's in May and am looking forward to working with the geriatric population in a different capacity but with the same heart and soul.

ADVANCED PRACTICE NURSING

Advanced practice nursing refers to four classifications of registered nurses with advanced education and experience who perform responsibilities once solely in the realm of physicians: nurse practitioners, clinical nurse specialists, nurse midwives, and nurse anesthetists. Most advanced practice nurses hold master's degrees, many prescribe medications, and all began their careers with the decision to become a nurse.

Historically, nurses obtained specialized education through hospital-based courses designed to provide knowledge in a specific area, usually obstetric and private-duty nursing. As the sciences advanced, nurses acquired greater knowledge of anatomy, physiology, microbiology, chemistry, pathophysiology, and pharmacology. They also increased their skills and assumed a more active role in client care. Knowledge that was once the sole domain of physicians crossed over to nursing—physical assessment, venipuncture, suturing, ordering diagnostic tests, and administering lifesaving medications under protocol. The more nurses' role expanded, the more specialized they became, requiring changes in standards of practice and formalized education.

Specialty master's nursing education evolved in colleges and universities in the 1940s ad 1950s. Military nurses returning home from World War II facilitated the idea because they often had GI benefits enabling them to return to school for advanced education. Passage of the National Mental Health Act of 1946 provided additional funds for psychiatric nurses, and the first clinical master's program to develop advanced practice psychiatric nurses was developed at Rutgers University in 1954.

The National League for Nurses sponsored a conference in 1952 where attendees agreed to a key issue that still holds today: The purpose of the baccalaureate degree is to prepare nurses as generalists, whereas master's education prepares them as specialists. Nursing envisioned master's education as the foundation for nurses in specialty practice. Early degrees, such as the master's offered at Columbia University in New York, focused on the role of the nurse as educator or administrator. During this time nurses with advanced practice degrees were called nurse clinicians or clinical nurse specialists, and their primary responsibility was to improve client care by acting as a nurse expert in an acute care setting.

The 1960s experienced a shortage and maldistribution of physicians, and in response to this issue, the University of Colorado developed the first nurse practitioner program, one that focused on pediatrics. Within nine years, there were 65 pediatric nurse practitioner programs in the United

States, as well as nurse practitioner programs in women's health and family health. However, because there was a lack of graduate degree programs, nurses created short-term certificate programs to develop nurse practitioners. Some required baccalaureate degrees, others did not; some were a few months in length; others were two years; and many had inconsistencies in prerequisites, program length, content, and goals.

Today, most advanced practice nursing education takes place at the graduate level, and the American Nurses Credentialing Center and other professional nursing organizations certify nurses who have obtained the appropriate education and experience. While the majority of advanced practice nurses have master's degrees, this, too, is changing. The new educational standard for 2015, though controversial, will be the Doctor of Nursing Practice, and universities across the nation already have programs in place or in the planning stage to convert to this degree.

The AACN *Essentials of Master's Education for Advanced Practice Nursing* defines the essential elements of master's education for advanced practice roles in nursing. As outlined in the *Essentials* document, the advanced practice master's curriculum has three components:

> The Graduate Nursing Core contains foundational curriculum essential for all master's students regardless of specialty or functional focus. This content includes: theoretical foundations of nursing practice; research; policy, organization, and financing of healthcare; ethics; professional role development; human diversity, and social issues; and health promotion and disease prevention.

> The Advanced Practice Nursing Core contains content essential for providing direct client services at the advanced level. This content includes advanced pathophysiology, advanced health assessment, and advanced pharmacology.

> The Specialty Curriculum Content focuses on those didactic and clinical learning experiences identified and defined by the specialty nursing organizations, such as the *Core Curriculum for Primary Care Pediatric Nurse Practitioners* by the National Association of Pediatric Nurse Practitioners and the Association of Faculties of Pediatric Nurse Practitioners.

Advanced Practice Nursing Core

All advanced practice nurses perform advanced clinical assessment and most prescribe medications; therefore, all require advanced pathophysiology, advanced physical assessment, and advanced pharmacology. These courses build on principles learned at the undergraduate level.

Advanced Pathophysiology

Advanced Pathophysiology utilizes principles from anatomy and physiology to provide nursing students with an advanced understanding of the pathophysiologic processes underlying human illness and disease entities across the life span, including their associated signs and symptoms and their appropriate laboratory data.

Advanced Clinical Assessment

This course combines lecture and practice to teach students how to obtain histories and perform comprehensive physical examinations on clients throughout the life span. Students practice their skills in the nursing laboratory and in the clinical setting.

Advanced Pharmacology

Advanced Pharmacology focuses on the principles of drug therapy, mechanisms of action, side effects, drug interactions, general concepts in the selection of pharmaceutical agents, as well as prescriptive authority.

Admission Requirements to Advance Practice Master's Programs

Admission requirements to advanced practice master's programs include: licensure as a registered nurse; a bachelor's degree in nursing and official transcripts from an accredited program; GPA of 3.0 or equivalent; and at least one year experience as a registered nurse (must be one year of critical care experience for nurse anesthesia programs).

Nurse Practitioner (NP)

Definition: The American College of Nurse Practitioners (ACNP) defines nurse practitioners (NPs) as registered nurses who have received graduate-level nursing education and clinical training, which enables them to provide a wide range of preventive and acute health care services to individuals of all ages. NPs obtain health histories and perform complete physical examinations; diagnose and treat many common acute and chronic problems; order and interpret laboratory and diagnostic tests; prescribe and manage medications and other therapies; provide health teaching and supportive counseling with an emphasis on prevention of illness and health maintenance; and refer patients to other health professionals as needed.

Standard of Practice: As with practical and registered nursing, each state defines its own standards for NPs, and these standards vary widely from state to state. An annual NP update called the "Pearson Report" appears in the February issues of *The American Journal for Nurse Practitioners*. This report supplies NPs with a state-by-state update on laws, rules, regulations, malpractice, and policy issues related to NPs. According to this report, states even differ on NP titles. Alabama and Pennsylvania use Certified Registered Nurse Practitioner (CRNP); Rhode Island and Utah use Registered Nurse Practitioner (RNP); Oregon, Tennessee, and New York use Nurse Practitioner (NP); Ohio and South Dakota use Certified Nurse Practitioner (CNP); California, Connecticut, and Vermont use Advanced Practice Registered Nurse (APRN); and Virginia uses Licensed Nurse Practitioner (LPN). Most states require NP certification to practice; those that don't include New York, North Dakota, and Oregon. And even though the AACN now recommends the DNP, some states (Delaware, Idaho, Indiana, Maryland, Minnesota, and New York, and the District of Columbia) still have no requirement for NPs to have master's degrees. Twenty-two states and the District of Columbia have no requirements for physician involvement for an NP to practice, four require physician involvement but no written protocol, and the remaining states require physician involvement with a written protocol. All states allow NPs to prescribe, but 39 require physician involvement. The abbreviated "Pearson Report" for 2008 can be retrieved at www.acnpweb.org/files/public/2008_Pearson_Report.pdf.

Practice Settings: Most Primary Care Nurse Practitioners (PCNPs) work in physicians' offices, clinics, schools, and occupational health clinics. While some hospital units and emergency centers employ primary care NPs, more of them are utilizing **Acute Care Nurse Practitioners (ACNPs)**, a relatively new NP role. All NPs specialize in a client population. PCNPs specialize in adult, family, pediatric, school, geriatric, and women's health nursing, as well as psychiatric mental health nursing. ACNPs may specialize in a client population, but many opt for a specific nursing area, such as cardiac care, trauma, pulmonology, or oncology.

Scope of Practice: Research demonstrates that **Primary Care Nurse Practitioners (PCNPs)** deliver competent and cost-effective primary care to clients across the life span. PCNPs perform wellness visit exams (checkups), order and interpret screening tests, administer immunizations, and provide health promotion teaching. They also diagnose and treat people who have acute problems such as ear infections, and chronic ones such as asthma. They prescribe medications and other treatments, see clients back for follow-up visits, and refer clients to specialists when needed. PCNPs perform procedures including suturing, casting, and skin biopsies.

Competencies: The National Organization of Nurse Practitioner Faculties (NONPF) and the AACN developed the *Nurse Practitioner Primary Care Competencies in Specialty Areas: Adult, Family, Gerontological, Pediatric and Women's Health*. These entry-level competencies are delineated for each specialty area and are intended to be used in conjunction with and build on the core competencies identified for all nurse practitioners. They can be accessed at www.nonpf.com/finalaug2002.pdf.

Practice Setting: Research demonstrates that **Acute Care Nurse Practitioners (ACNPs)** provide quality care, decrease length of stay, and improve patient and family satisfaction. They assess and manage acutely ill patients within the inpatient/hospital setting, as well as in the emergency department, intensive care unit, specialty labs, acute care wards, specialty clinics, or any combination of these.

Scope of Practice: ACNPs can diagnose and treat medical conditions, and many provide direct client management from admission to discharge, in collaboration with physicians and other members of the healthcare team. Some ACNPs continue to care for clients into the outpatient setting to ensure successful transition after discharge and complete resolution of transitioning their needs. The exact nature and structure of the ACNP role depends on the collaborative agreement with physicians and other members of the healthcare team.

Competencies: The NONPF National Panel for Acute Care Nurse Practitioner Competencies developed the Acute Care Nurse Practitioner Competencies. These entry-level competencies are intended to be used in conjunction with and build on the core competencies identified for all nurse practitioners. This document may be accessed at www.aacn.nche.edu/ Education/pdf/ACNPcompsfinal2004.pdf.

Many states require that NPs be certified in their specialty area. To attain certification, NPs must have graduated from an accredited graduate-level nurse practitioner program, successfully pass a certification exam to verify knowledge in their specialty, and pay a fee. NPs are expected to maintain their certification by demonstrating continued competency in their specialty through clinical practice, continuing nursing education, completing academic courses, completing self-assessment modules, publishing in peer-reviewed journals, presenting at nursing conferences, and/or taking another exam. Agencies that certify nurse practitioners are:

▶ The American Nurses Credentialing Center certifies family, adult, pediatric, school nurse, acute care, diabetes management, adult psychiatric mental health, and family psychiatric mental health nurse practitioners.

▶ The Pediatric Nursing Certification Board certifies pediatric primary care nurse practitioners and pediatric acute care nurse practitioners.

▶ The American Academy of Nurse Practitioners certifies family, adult, and gerontological nurse practitioners.

Clinical Nurse Specialist

Definition: The National Association of Clinical Nurse Specialists defines Clinical Nurse Specialists (CNS) as expert clinicians in a specialized area of nursing practice that may be a population (such as children or older adults), a setting (such as dialysis or critical care), a disease or subspecialty (such as HIV/AIDS or orthopedics), a care type (such as palliative care or rehabilitation), or a specific problem (such as pain or cardiac rehabilitation). All CNSs focus on five areas: clinical practice, teaching, research, consulting, and management.

CNSs are also prepared as case managers who organize and coordinate client services and resources, controlling costs in the interim. Therefore, they are invaluable in managed care. Their educational role covers patient, nursing, and other staff education, as well as community education, and the teaching and precepting of nursing students.

The role of the CNS is not without controversy due to its similarities with the NP role and more recently that of the clinical nurse leader. In 1994 AACN held a conference on role differentiation to decide whether the two roles should remain separate or be blended. The reasons for blending the roles were: less confusion for the public; clarification of titles and competencies; increased political and professional power; greater marketability; guaranteeing that advanced practice nurses would be prepared at the master's level; and increased benefits to clients. Sixty-eight percent of the group voted to merge the two roles, and schools began the process. But as you can see here, the merger never happened.

In 2006, AACN issued a statement noting its support of the CNS role. Citing its awareness of the direct link between graduate-prepared nurses and both patient safety and positive outcomes, AACN supported the definition of the CNS as outlined by the American Nurses Association's 2004 *Nursing: Scope and Standards of Practice* and stated that CNSs play a unique role in the delivery of high-quality nursing care. CNSs are experts in evidence-based nursing and practice in a range of specialty areas. In addition to direct patient care, they teach, mentor, consult, research, manage and improve systems, and are adept at adapting their practice across settings. CNSs provide expert consultation to all care providers and implement improvements in healthcare delivery systems. AACN recognized the growing body of evidence that shows a strong correlation between CNS interventions and safe, cost-effective patient care. CNSs reduce hospital costs and lengths of stay, reduce frequency of emergency room visits, improve pain management practices, increase patient satisfaction with nursing care, and minimize complications in hospitalized patients. Thus, AACN encourages hospitals and other healthcare providers to use CNSs and engage them in the health arena. AACN further stated that CNSs do not duplicate the role of Clinical Nurse Leaders, who are educated as generalists, while CNSs are educated as specialists.

Standards of Practice: State nurse practice acts govern standards of practice for clinical nurse specialists. Since some CNSs prescribe medications, their standards are similar to nurse practitioners, thus some states require physician involvement, while others do not. States also accept and incorporate the standards of the National Association of Clinical Nurse Specialists (NACNS) *Statement on CNS Practice and Education*, and the AACN *Essentials of Masters Education for Advanced Practice*.

Practice Settings: While many CNSs practice in hospitals, others practice in a variety of settings. Additional settings include long-term care, cancer treatment centers, renal dialysis centers, and rehabilitation facilities.

Scope of Practice: CNS practice focuses on five areas: clinical practice, teaching, research, consulting, and management. As experts in clinical practice, CNSs work with other healthcare professionals to improve client care. They assess and intervene with complex health problems within their specialty area, using appropriate technology, products, and devices. CNSs educate other staff and precept nursing students. They use research to create evidence-based practice, and perform consultative functions in multiple health settings. As leaders, they act as change agents by developing healthcare standards, assisting in the implementation of standards, facilitating goal setting and achievement, and evaluating outcomes. CNSs also serve as leaders in the community to better overall health care.

Competencies: The National Association of Clinical Nurse Specialists (NACNS) determined required competencies in their document, the *NACNS Statement on CNS Practice and Education*. This statement defines CNS practice competencies and makes recommendations for CNS education, and is available at www.nacns.org/statement.shtml.

Certification: CNSs can obtain certification by examination in some, but not all, specialties. ANCC offers credentialing for CNSs in the following specialties: adult health, pediatric, child and adolescent psychiatric and mental health, adult psychiatric and mental health, diabetes management, gerontological, home health, and public and community health. ANCC and

NACNS are presently addressing a barrier to practice faced by a number of CNSs, the lack of a certification exam in many specialties. State boards of nursing often require national certification for practice. Since certification is available for a limited number of specialties, ANCC, working in collaboration with NACNS, is developing a CNS core certification examination that will test the competencies required of all CNSs regardless of their specialty. ANCC expects this exam to be available in September 2009.

Some specialty nursing organizations offer certification for CNSs. The Oncology Nursing Certification Corporation (www.oncc.org) offers Oncology CNS certification. The American Association of Critical Care Nurses Certification Corporation (www.certcorp.org) offers the Critical Care Nurse Specialist certification, and the Orthopaedic Nurses Certification Board (www.oncb.org) offers Orthopedic CNS certification.

Psychiatric Nurse Practitioners and Clinical Specialists

Advanced practice psychiatric nurses provide comprehensive mental health care to individuals, groups, and families across the life span. An advanced practice psychiatric nurse may function as a clinical nurse specialist, nurse practitioner, or, in some cases, both, since they are very similar in this specialty area. As previously noted, Psychiatric Mental Health Clinical Nurse Specialists (PMHCNS) were the first advanced practice nurses in the United States. Their role today consists of five domains: research, clinical leadership, education, consultation, and expert clinical practice, but their practice emphasis may vary. The scope of practice for PMHCNSs can include psychotherapy practice as well as staff development.

Psychiatric Mental Health Nurse Practitioners (PMHNPs) primarily practice in a clinical setting, diagnosing psychiatric disorders and utilizing a range of interventions that include medications, individual therapy, family therapy, group therapy, and behavioral therapy. Both clinical nurse specialists and nurse practitioners practice with a defined patient population (such as adults, elders, or children and adolescents) or a specific problem, such as eating disorders or substance abuse, and both work in a variety of settings, including: inpatient psychiatric units, emergent or urgent psychiatric centers, outpatient services, private practices, and psychiatric consultation liaison services (with medically ill clients). They may also work as specialists in settings such as jail health services, high-risk pregnancy clinics, schools, substance abuse centers, and recovery programs.

NONPF's National Panel for Psychiatric-Mental Health NP Competencies developed the *Psychiatric Mental-Health Nurse Competencies*, a document that emphasizes the unique philosophy of practice for the psychiatric-mental health nurse practitioner specialty and the needs of the populations served. These entry-level competencies apply to all Psychiatric Mental Health NPs regardless of the population they serve and are intended to be used in conjunction with and build on the core competencies identified for all nurse practitioners. This document can be accessed at www.aacn.nche.edu/Accreditation/psychiatricmentalhealthnursepractitionercopetencies/FINAL03.pdf.

Nurse Midwife

Definition: According to the American College of Nurse Midwives, nurse midwives are advanced practice nurses with additional training to deliver babies and provide prenatal and postpartum care to women. Nurse midwives are so involved in labor and delivery that they sometimes do not leave the mother during the entire labor process. They are trained to recognize signs of complications and will consult with a physician to become involved in the delivery if needed. Nurse midwives qualify to administer medications and perform procedures; however, they use these only when requested by the mother.

Nurse midwives differ from lay midwives, who are now known as direct-entry midwives. Nurse midwives are registered nurses with advanced practice education. While some direct-entry midwives may be nurses, they are not advanced practice nurses. Direct-entry midwives are independent practitioners educated in the discipline of midwifery through self-study, apprenticeship, a midwifery school, or a college- or university-based program distinct from the discipline of nursing. They are trained to provide the Midwives Model of Care to healthy women and newborns throughout the childbearing cycle, primarily in out-of-hospital settings. The American College of Nurse Midwives offers Certified Midwife (CM) designation for lay midwives who graduate from a midwifery school accredited by the ACNM, and pass a certification exam.

To become a certified nurse midwife (CNM) you must graduate from a nurse midwifery program accredited by the American College of Nurse Midwives, and pass a national certification exam. CNMs can practice anywhere in the United States. Some states require national certification for licensed CNMs to practice midwifery. Don't rule out this specialty if you're male; approximately 2 percent of CNMs are men.

Standards of Practice: Each state sets its own standards for the practice and regulation of nurse midwifery. Prescriptive authority is an issue, as it is for other advanced practice nurses, with the addition of intrapartum prescriptive and administrative authority. The ACNM provides fact sheets for each state at www.acnm.org/state_legislation.cfm. These individual fact sheets outline practice and reimbursement, as well as statistics, education, and an overview of nurse midwives.

Practice Settings: Nurse midwives practice in homes, birth centers, hospitals, private practice, state and county health departments, and charitable organizations.

Scope of Practice: Nurse midwives provide prenatal care, birthing, postpartum care, gynecologic exams, treatment of sexually transmitted diseases, birth control, and contraception (birth control), which includes injections, implants, intrauterine devices (IUDs), birth control pills, and diaphragms. Nurse midwives provide primary healthcare to women from menarche through menopause and beyond, as well as health teaching on issues including natural childbirth, teen pregnancy, and breast-feeding.

Competencies: The *Core Competencies for Basic Midwifery Practice* describes the fundamental knowledge, skills, and behaviors expected of a new practitioner. They may be accessed at www.midwife.org/display.cfm?id=484.

Certification: The American Midwifery Certification Board (AMCB), formerly the ACNM Certification Council, Inc. (ACC) is the national certifying body for Certified Nurse-Midwives (CNMs). They can be accessed at www.amcbmidwife.org.

NURSING NOTES

A Lesson on Nurse Midwifery, by Nicole Rouhana

Nurse midwifery is a privilege that allows me to participate in the most intimate aspects of health and reproduction a woman experiences. This glimpse into the most private recesses of a women's soul allows me to be with women whether they are profoundly happy or terribly sad. I have had women call me after the death of a loved one, just to share the news with somebody they had a connection with despite the fact it had nothing to do with their healthcare. Sometimes we care for women who do not share our same values or lifestyles but we still support, educate respectfully, and help them to make the best decisions they can regarding their reproductive health.

But what does it actually mean to be a nurse midwife? It means long hours that require a huge commitment, missing important family events and holidays, missing regular hours of sleep on a routine basis, and a call schedule that can sometimes interfere with life in general. It means caring for women living on the fringes of society, struggling to make ends meet and doing the best they can for themselves and their family, often forgotten or overlooked by society. It means hearing stories of abuse, shared for the first time, as nobody else had ever bothered to ask. Conversely, it also means being with a mother when she hears her baby's heart for the first time, helping a new mother nurse her baby for the first time after a long labor, and watching as a new family emerges from the shadows of a semilit labor room, or witnessing the profound empowerment that develops in a woman who has been an active participant at her birth and realizes that she alone could do this for her baby. Midwifery for me is a true work of art grounded in science.

Some of the most memorable lessons I have learned in nurse midwifery practice have come from some of the poorest, most disenfranchised women I have cared for. These lessons were not intentional, but rather were examples of fortitude and perseverance they showed me. One such memory involved a young woman named Phyllis. She had an infant who was born with a disability that would not be cured or improved, but rather worsened over time. She had recently relocated to my area from the Midwest and found herself pregnant for a second time. The young father of the baby had grown weary of responsibility and was no longer in the picture. Because she had a limited support system, she and I developed a relationship over her 40 weeks of prenatal care. As the child had grown too big to physically carry, she wheeled him around, bringing him to each prenatal visit. During her labor, we received a phone call from the neighbor caring for her child at home. The child had begun seizing, which was somewhat routine, and was taken to the emergency room at the same hospital. As the labor progressed, the child's seizures continued, beyond what they had ever been before. After a few hours a neurologist was called in who recommended anesthesia to control the seizures. The risk associated with this treatment was that the child might not resume consciousness and the seizures could no longer be controlled medically. Phyllis and I discussed this in between contractions and she consented. The labor continued and within the next few hours she delivered a health baby girl uneventfully. At six hours post partum Phyllis and

I went to the ICU to visit her son, who continued to seize under anesthesia. A storm raged outside on this hot summer night and I stood at the window and watched the silent bolts of lightning flash in heavy humid air, listening to the cardiac monitor regularly beeping behind the curtain as Phyllis crooned comforting words to her son. "Mommy is here, Kenny. Guess what? We have a new baby sister and she is healthy and beautiful. It's okay to go now . . . she's here, Mommy is okay, now you rest and go to sleep." Within half an hour the cardiac monitor began to sound irregular beats, pausing for longer intervals, as Kenny's heart began to fail. The storm raged on as Phyllis continued quietly talking. By 2 A.M. we sat and held her son's lifeless body, finally at peace and seizure-free. His journey had come to an end. A soft and gentle quiet rain had moved in after the storm as the outside temperature dropped. I will always remember the intrinsic connection that night between mother and son. I am grateful that I was privileged to have been part of that process.

Nurse Anesthetist

Definition: The American Association of Nurse Anesthetists (AANA) define nurse anesthetists (also known as certified registered nurse anesthetists or CRNAs) as anesthesia professionals who safely administer approximately 30 million anesthetics to clients each year. The credential of CRNA first existed in 1956, and research indicates that nurse anesthetists provide the same quality of care as that provided by their physician counterparts. Regardless of whether they are physicians or nurses, all anesthesia professionals give anesthesia the same way.

Nurse anesthesia is a popular advanced practice role because of its independence and salary. It is also a popular choice of male nurses. Approximately 44 percent of all nurse anesthetists and student nurse anesthetists are men, compared with less than 10 percent in the nursing profession as a whole.

Standards of Practice: The AANA Scope and Standards of Practice acts as a guide for nurse anesthetists and healthcare providers regarding nurse anesthetist practice (www.aana.com/uploadedFiles/Resources/Practice_Documents/scope_stds_nap07_2007.pdf). As with other areas of nursing, state nurse practice acts guide and regulate the practice of nurse anesthetists. Some nurse practice acts specifically limit the administration of anesthetics to nurse anesthetists. State summaries are found at www.aana.com/Resources .aspx?ucNavMenu_TSMenuTargetID=52&ucNavMenu_TSMenuTarget Type=4&ucNavMenu_TSMenuID=6&id=798.

Practice Settings: Nurse anesthetists provide anesthesia in collaboration with surgeons, anesthesiologists, dentists, podiatrists, and other qualified healthcare professionals. Nurse anesthetists practice in every setting where anesthesia is delivered: hospitals; ambulatory surgical centers; the offices of dentists, podiatrists, ophthalmologists, plastic surgeons, and pain management specialists; and the U.S. military, Public Health Services, and Department of Veterans Affairs healthcare facilities. Nurse anesthetists have been the main providers of anesthesia care to U.S. military men and women on the front lines from World War I through the conflict in Iraq, but they first provided anesthesia to wounded soldiers during the Civil War.

Nurse anesthetists are the primary anesthesia providers in rural areas, enabling healthcare facilities in these medically underserved areas to offer obstetrical, surgical, and trauma stabilization services to their local communities. In some states, nurse anesthetists are the only anesthesia providers in nearly 100 percent of the rural hospitals.

Scope of Practice: Nurse anesthetists care for clients' anesthesia needs before, during, and after surgery or the delivery of a baby. They perform physical assessments and participate in preoperative teaching. Nurse anesthetists prepare for anesthetic management, administer anesthesia to keep clients pain-free, and maintain anesthesia intraoperatively. They also oversee clients' recovery from anesthesia and follow the client's postoperative course from recovery room to the client care unit.

Competencies: AANA has already mobilized and created a doctoral level competency document for nurse anesthetists. This may be accessed at www.aana.com/uploadedFiles/Professional_Development/Nurse_Anesthesia_ Education/Educational_Resources/DTF_Report/competencies.pdf.

Certification: The National Board on Certification and Recertification of Nurse Anesthetists (NBCRNA) certifies nurse anesthetists as CRNAs, while the Council on Certification of Nurse Anesthetists oversees recertification.

INDIRECT PRACTICE GRADUATE EDUCATION

While all nursing roles have some clinical component, these graduate level roles have other primary purposes. Nurse educators teach; nurse executives lead; and nurse researchers conduct research.

Nurse Educator

Definition: Nurse educators incorporate teaching, mentoring, research, and client care into one role. Nurse educators are responsible for affecting the quality of client care whether they are educating nursing students or improving the competence and advancement of practicing nurses. Nurse educators develop lesson plans, teaching tools, and evaluation methods. They teach in class or group settings and on a one-to-one basis to assist students and staff in solving learning problems. Many nurse educators act as consultants.

Education: Education varies significantly. Many nurse educators were educated as advanced practice nurses, while others received their master's in nursing education. Teaching at the baccalaureate or higher level typically requires a doctorate if the nurse educator desires a tenure track position. Doctorates also vary. The majority of doctorally prepared nurse educators hold a doctor of philosophy degree (PhD), while others have a doctor of education (EdD) or doctor of nursing science (DNS). More recently, nurses teach with doctor of nursing practice degrees (DNP). While this is a practice doctorate and not intended as a teaching degree, there are nurse educators who received it.

Practice Setting: Nurse educators work as instructors or faculty, teaching nursing students at all levels: practical, diploma, associate, baccalaureate, master's, and doctoral in educational settings. They also work in a variety of settings—hospitals, long-term care, veterans centers, and clinics—providing practicing nurses with continuing education and staff development.

Scope of Practice: All nurse educators teach, but their scope of practice depends on their position. Nurses who teach in practical, diploma, associate, and baccalaureate programs usually teach more than their own specialty, regardless of their background. For example, a pediatric nurse educator may teach the pediatric lecture and clinical in the fall, then women's health clinical in the spring. Nurse educators who teach at the graduate level tend to have a more focused teaching assignment. However, nurses who teach advanced clinical courses need to maintain an active nursing practice of their own. Master's and doctoral faculty also participate on master's thesis and doctoral dissertation committees.

Most faculty members participate in committee work and advise students. Tenure track faculty are also expected to engage in scholarship, which consists of research, publications, and presentations. Other nontenured faculty members teach only clinical practicums and do not participate in scholarship unless they choose to participate. Adjunct faculty work part-time and usually teach clinical practicums.

Types of Teaching Appointments

Tenure Track	Nontenure Track	Adjunct
Tenure equates to a permanent job contract	Contract position	Contract position
Takes 6–7 years to earn tenure	Contract renewed every 1–3 years	Temporary and usually part-time
Doctorate required	Doctorate not usually required	Doctorate not required
Teaching, scholarship, and service expected	Teaching is main focus	Teaching is the only focus
Ranks: assistant professor, associate professor, professor	Ranks: clinical instructor, clinical associate professor, clinical professor, clinical assistant professor	No ranks
Number of positions limited in each college/university	Number of positions variable	Multiple positions to teach practicums
Some schools are replacing tenure with annual contracts	More schools adding nontenure track positions	Most schools use adjuncts
Positives: job security, support for scholarship	Positive: usually less stressful than tenure track	Positives: flexible scheduling, creates a way to see if you like teaching
Negative: can be difficult to attain tenure	Negative: less job security	Negative: no job security

Staff development educators provide nonacademic learning activities intended to build on the educational and experiential bases of professional nurses and other health care personnel. Staff development educators design these learning activities to enhance nursing practice, education, administration, research, or theory development with the goal of improving client health.

Certification: The National League for Nurses provides a certification opportunity for nursing faculty through examination. To sit for the exam, nurse educators must meet one of two options. For option one, they must have a master's or doctoral degree in nursing with a major emphasis in nursing education and two or more years of full-time employment in the academic faculty role within the past five years. Option two requires the nurse educator to hold a master's or doctoral degree in nursing with an emphasis on a role other than education and four or more years of full-time employment in the academic faculty role within the past five years. Both options require that the nurse educator be licensed as a registered nurse.

Staff development educators may obtain certification from the American Nurses Credentialing Center. To be eligible for the credentialing exam, nurses must be licensed as an RN, hold a baccalaureate or higher degree in nursing, have a minimum of 4,000 hours of practice in nursing professional development within the previous five years, and have completed 30 hours of continuing education in nursing professional development within the past five years.

Nurse Executive

Definition: According to the American Organization of Nurse Executives (AONE) nurse executives are described as nurses who design, facilitate, and manage care. The elements of nurse executive practice include networks of care providers, collaboration among health professionals, partnerships with consumers, collective accountability, advocacy for those who cannot advocate for themselves, and leadership in cost-effective client care.

Education: They must have solid leadership and management skills, as well as critical thinking, decision-making, and communication skills. Therefore, the role of nurse executive requires graduation from an accredited school with a master's degree in nursing administration or in hospital or business administration. Small agencies consider equivalent experience in lieu of the degree.

Practice Setting: Nurse executive areas include management and administration. Nurse executives practice in hospitals and schools of nursing, and as independent consultants. Many are directors of nursing, others are vice presidents. Some work as chief executive officers (CEOs). Specialty hospitals may prefer nurse executives with clinical experience in that specialty field.

Scope of Practice: Nurse executive are responsible for managing organized nursing services. They collaborate with other healthcare executives to make decisions about healthcare services and organizational priorities. Nurse executives ensure the implementation of standards of nursing practice, and that these standards are consistent with those of professional organizations and regulatory agencies. Nurse executives evaluate care delivery models and the services provided to individuals and groups, and they foster an atmosphere for practice that enhances job satisfaction, productivity, and professional development.

Certification: Nurse executives have options for certification. They may pursue ANCC certification as a nurse executive, provided they meet the criteria: license as a registered nurse; master's degree or higher in nursing or a related field; hold an administrative position at the executive level or a faculty position teaching graduate executive level nursing students for at least 24 months full-time; completed 30 hours of continuing education in nursing administration within the last three years.

Nurse executives can choose certification through the AONE as either Certified in Executive Nursing Practice (CENP) or Certified Nurse Manager and Leader (CNML). CENP focuses on those engaged in executive nursing practice. Eligibility criteria include a license as a registered nurse and a master's or higher degree (one degree must be in nursing) plus two years of experience in the executive role, or a bachelor's degree in nursing plus four years in the executive role. CNML, offered in partnership with the American Association of Critical Care Nurses, focuses exclusively on leaders in the nurse manager role. Eligibility criteria include a nursing license as a registered nurse; a bachelor's degree or higher in nursing plus two years of experience with a minimum of 1,040 hours per year as a nurse manager; or a non-nursing bachelor's degree plus three years of experience with a minimum of 1,040 hours per year in a nurse manager role; or an RN diploma or associate degree plus five years of experience with a minimum of 1,040 hours per year in a nurse manager role. While not an executive certification, the CNML may act as a stepping-stone, and it provides a managerial certification for those registered nurses with diploma or associate degrees.

Nurse Researcher

Definition: According to the National Institute for Nursing Research (NINR), nursing research develops knowledge to build the scientific foundation for clinical practice, prevent disease and disability, manage and eliminate illness symptoms, and enhance end-of-life care. While many nurses conduct research as part of their job, especially nursing faculty and advanced practice nurses, nurse researchers do little else.

Education: Nurse researchers typically hold a doctorate degree, usually a PhD.

Practice Setting: Nurse researchers work for private companies and not-for-profit organizations.

Scope of Practice: Nurse researchers conduct research on their own, with other nurses, or in collaboration with other disciplines, including medicine, pharmacy, and the social sciences. They design studies, collect clinical data, analyze results, and draw conclusions and recommendations. They publish their results in peer-reviewed journals. Nurse researchers also write and manage grants to fund their research.

Certification: There is no certification process for nurse researchers at this point.

THE NURSING DOCTORATE

The thought of "Doctor Nurse" may sound peculiar, but the word "doctor" is not reserved for physicians. Dentists are doctors, so are veterinarians and optometrists. Nurses can be doctors, too—Doctors of Philosophy (PhD) or Doctors of Nursing Practice (DNP).

Getting that doctorate may be the last thing on your mind as you contemplate whether you even want to be a nurse. However, once you make that decision, think about where you want to be five years from now.

Nursing needs doctorally prepared nurses, and need creates opportunity, including accelerated programs, such as the BSN to PhD or BSN to DNP. Five years from now, you can be taking doctoral courses.

Doctor of Philosophy (PhD) in Nursing

If you plan a career in nursing education or research, aim for the PhD. The PhD prepares nurse scientists and scholars, researchers, and educators. Educational programs focus heavily on theory, meta-theory, statistics, and research methodology with one or two courses on healthcare policy, healthcare systems, and/or nursing issues. Courses usually culminate in the completion of a dissertation, which is a research project. Your dissertation will probably take a year or more to complete, so make sure you choose a topic that not only interests you but that is also doable in a reasonable period of time. Your dissertation is important, but it is not your life's work. You do your life's work after you get your PhD.

Doctor of Nursing Practice (DNP)

If you want a career in advanced practice or administration, set your sights on the DNP. AACN proposes the DNP as the entry-level degree for all advanced practice nursing roles—nurse practitioner, clinical nurse specialist, nurse midwife, and nurse anesthetist—by 2015. Where will you be five years from now? With accelerated programs, whether you're a high school senior or a retiree, you can be moving toward completion of your DNP five years from now.

The DNP is the practice doctorate. Today's complex health system requires well-educated professionals. Nurses with DNPs are needed to evaluate and deliver evidence-based care, set health policy, lead and manage healthcare units and systems, develop interdisciplinary standards, solve healthcare dilemmas, and reduce healthcare delivery disparities. They would be prepared and credentialed as independent practitioners just like doctors of pharmacy, doctors of clinical psychology, doctors of physical therapy, and doctors of medicine. States may continue to mandate an advanced-practice nurse/physician relationship, but the premise of the DNP is that the graduate would not require specific physician ties. Instead, nurses with DNPs would be fully accountable for their own practice and would collaborate with all healthcare specialists.

While the PhD focuses on theory and research, the DNP focuses on practice and leadership. Courses culminate in an evidence-based project. Like the dissertation, this, too, is a time-consuming and rigorous ordeal, so choose a topic that feeds your passion.

Differences between the PhD and the DNP

PhD	DNP
Research-focused	Practice-focused
Courses on theory, statistics, research	Courses on evidence-based practice, leadership, informatics
Dissertation	Evidence-based practice project
Generates nursing knowledge	Applies nursing knowledge

Nursing needs doctorally prepared faculty and doctorally prepared practitioners. Remember, the need for nursing means opportunity for you. If you see yourself moving ahead in your career, plan now. People who enter baccalaureate programs are four times more likely to pursue graduate education than those who enter nursing at the diploma or associate degree level. But today's mobility programs, even LPN-BSN, can help change that trend. However, choose your entry point wisely and pay attention to accreditation and articulation. Entry-level programs accredited by the Commission on Collegiate Nursing Education and the National League for Nursing Accrediting Commission meet professional standards, and thus meet admission criteria for graduate-level programs. They also transfer in mobility programs. If time or money affects your decision today, look into practical, diploma, or associate degree programs that have articulation agreements with baccalaureate programs. Articulation agreements ease the credit transfer between institutions. The more credits you transfer, the faster you graduate.

Many universities offer their PhD and DNP programs online, saving you travel money and easing your schedule juggling. PhD programs have been around for a long time, but DNP programs are proliferating, so you have plenty of options to choose from. Google "online nursing PhD and DNP programs" and see what the future may hold for you.

CHAPTER **five**

LICENSURE, CERTIFICATION, AND CONTINUING EDUCATION

LICENSURE

The Merriam-Webster dictionary defines a license as permission granted by a competent authority to engage in an activity or business that is otherwise unlawful. License comes from the Latin word *licēre*, which means "to be permitted." A license gives you the freedom to act.

Both registered and practical nurses need to be licensed to practice nursing. Licensure assists in assuring that nurses meet the minimum requirements to safely practice in the state or states in which they maintain licensure.

Requirements for Licensure

While some states allow you to work for a brief period (usually about 60 days) prior to your passing your licensure exam, others do not, and no state allows you to work as a nurse for any substantial amount of time without a license. Although requirements may vary per state, the minimum requirements for licensure as either a practical nurse or a registered nurse are:

▶ completing a license application

▶ graduating from, or verification of completion and eligibility for graduation from, a state-approved nursing program

▶ passing the National Council Licensure Examination for Practical Nurses (NCLEX-PN) or the National Council Licensure Examination for Registered Nurses (NCLEX-RN)

▶ self-reporting of all felony convictions and plea agreements, as well as misdemeanor conviction of lesser included offenses arising from felony arrests. Local/state and federal background checks using current technology, such as fingerprinting, are performed to validate the self-report. Court documents, including the disposition of all cases, are usually required for candidates with criminal histories. Each state handles the presence of a criminal history differently, so you will need to check with your state board of nursing to see how you may be affected if you have a criminal history.

▶ self-reporting of any drug-related behavior that can impair the licensure candidate's ability to provide safe care. Each state handles drug-related behavior differently, so you will need to check with your state board of nursing to see how you may be affected if you have a criminal history.

▶ self-reporting of any functional ability deficit that requires accommodation to perform essential nursing functions

▶ paying licensure fees (some states do not accept personal checks and only accept certified bank checks or money orders)

Other possible requirements, depending on the state or territory where the license candidate plans to work:

▶ minimum of at least 18 years of age (minimum may be 17 years of age for practical nurses)

▶ completion of the twelfth grade of schooling or its equivalent

▶ inclusion of 2″ × 2″ passport-type photo with license application

▶ transcripts from completed nursing program

▶ copy of your high school diploma (required by some states for practical nursing licensure)

▶ notarization of licensure application

▶ completion of state-mandated coursework or training, which may include coursework or training on child abuse, elder abuse, and/or intimate partner violence (domestic violence)

To learn about your state nursing licensure requirements, contact your state board of nursing, which can be found in Appendix A.

Temporary Permits

Some states allow first-time licensure applicants to work as a graduate nurse (GN). To do this, you may request a temporary permit to practice nursing. The permit is issued on approval of the completed licensure application. Permits are nonrenewable, last for about 90 days to six months (depending on the state where the permit is obtained), and expire when a nursing license is either approved by passing the NCLEX examination or when a nursing license is disapproved due to failing the NCLEX exam. To be eligible for a temporary permit, applicants must have never failed the NCLEX exam and never failed to appear and take the exam.

Temporary permits allow graduate nurses to practice under the direct supervision of a currently licensed registered nurse who is physically present in the facility and accessible to designate or prescribe a course of action when performing complex or advanced skills. Graduate nurses working under temporary permits must notify their employer immediately upon notice of failure to pass the NLCEX exam or licensure disapproval.

The Licensure Exam

State and territorial boards of nursing regulate nursing practice and help to ensure public safety by requiring that candidates for nursing licensure pass an examination that measures the competencies needed to perform safely and effectively as an entry-level nurse. Once a license is issued, the board of nursing continues to monitor the nurse's compliance with state laws and takes action against those nurses who exhibit unsafe nursing practice.

Each state determines membership of their board of nursing, but most include a mix of registered nurses, licensed practical nurses, advanced practice nurses, and consumers, all of whom were appointed to their positions. The boards of nursing in all 50 states, the District of Columbia, Guam, the Virgin Islands, American Samoa, and the Northern Mariana Islands make up the membership of the National Council of State Boards of Nursing (NCSBN).

The NCBSN has two licensure examinations that are used by state and territorial boards of nursing to assist them in making licensure decisions. These exams are the National Council Licensure Examination for Practical Nurses (NCLEX-PN) and the National Council Licensure Examination for Registered Nurses (NCLEX-RN). The NCLEX exams test knowledge, skills, and abilities for the safe and effective practice of nursing at the entry level. The NCLEX exams are administered by Computer Adaptive Testing (CAT). You take the exam on a computer, but you do not have to have computer skills to take it. The exam comes with a tutorial that demonstrates how to use the mouse and the on-screen calculator, how to record your answers, and the various question formats. One the exam begins, you will be able to request assistance on how to use the computer.

Persons diagnosed as having a disability and who require special testing accommodations may submit a "Request for Reasonable Testing Accommodations" form and appropriate documentation.

Since the NCLEX is a computerized test, it is true that not everyone gets the same test. Each of your test items is specifically chosen for you based on the answer you give to the previous question. The test program gives you questions with the degree of difficulty based on your ability, and it continues to do this until it becomes apparent that your ability is either above or below the passing standard. Therefore, some candidates may complete the minimum number of questions and pass, while others complete the minimum and fail—the computer shuts off the test once it is evident whether you pass or fail.

Based on your ability level, you may receive anywhere from 75 to 265 questions with a six-hour maximum time period for completion for the NCLEX-RN, or 85 to 205 questions within a five-hour maximum for the NCLEX-PN. Try to give yourself about one minute per question to keep within the time limit—you will be used to this because most of your nursing program exams were developed with that time frame in mind. The computer allows you two prescheduled breaks over the five/six hours. You may take these breaks or opt out. The test ends when you answered enough questions to show that you passed or failed, completed the maximum number of questions, or reached the maximum time. You pass if you demonstrate that you achieve a competence measure above the passing standard. You do not pass if you achieve a competence measure below the passing standard or if you answer fewer than the required minimum number of questions before the maximum time expires.

NCLEX questions appear one at a time. You can spend as much time as you like on each (keeping that 5/6 hour maximum in mind), but you cannot backtrack to previous questions. You can also change your answer until you confirm your answer to move on to the next question.

You will need your critical thinking cap to take NCLEX, as the majority of items (questions) are written in a manner targeted to the higher levels of cognitive function. That means you will be asked to apply, analyze, synthesize, and evaluate. Essentially, you will need to know what to do in given situations. Make sure you read the question carefully and that you do not add your own information to it.

The content focuses on client needs: management of care, safety, infection control, health promotion and maintenance, basic care and comfort, pharmacological and parenteral therapies, reduction of risk potential, physiological adaptation, and psychological integrity. There are some content differences between the NCLEX-RN and the NCLEX-PN. The NCLEX-RN will expect RN candidates to prioritize patients and to assign tasks to practical nurses and nursing assistants, while the NCLEX-PN will expect LPN candidates to request more assistance from registered nurses and to assign tasks to nursing assistants.

Most test items are traditional four-option, multiple choice questions. But alternative items may include multiple answers (multiple choice questions that require the licensure candidate to select one or more responses), fill-in-the-blanks, and items that require the test-taker to identify an area on a picture or graphic (sometimes called "hot spots"). All item formats may include graphics, tables, or charts.

Four-option multiple choice items contain the stem (question) and four answer choices. You choose only one of the options.

> A $3\frac{1}{2}$-year-old child is hospitalized with a fractured femur and placed in a full body cast. In the plan of care, the nurse should include developmental enhancing activities that include:
>
> a. building a tower with blocks
> b. collecting dolls or toy cars
> c. noisy pull toys
> d. puppets for a puppet show

The correct answer is d. A three-and-one-half-year-old child is a preschooler, and preschoolers require imaginative play to enhance their development. When choosing diversional activities for children, think development as well as diagnosis. A child in a full body cast will not be able to run around and play!

Multiple answer items contain a stem and a list of possible answers. For these you may choose as many options that you find appropriate.

> A patient with chronic obstructive pulmonary disease (COPD) has been receiving oxygen therapy for an extended time. The nurse suspects that the patient is experiencing oxygen toxicity as evidenced by:
>
> substernal discomfort
> paresthesia
> malaise
> fatigue
> dyspnea
> restlessness

The correct response for this question is to choose all of these answers because all of them are signs of oxygen toxicity. Oxygen is essential for life, but certain clients can develop oxygen toxicity if exposed to high concentrations for a brief period of time or low concentration over a prolonged period of time. Read multiple answer items carefully because one, some, or all of the answers may be correct.

Fill-in-the-blank questions require you to type in your response. Many of these are dosage calculation items that test both your math and formula skills.

> The nurse needs to administer Amoxicillin 250 mg. Amoxicillin comes in 500 mg per 5 ml. The nurse should administer _____ ml.

> The correct answer is 2.5ml.
> 500 mg = 5ml. The nurse needs to administer 250 mg.
> Cross multiply 500/5ml : 250/x
> $500x = 1,250 = 1,250/500 = 2.5$

Dosage calculation questions are common on NCLEX—and exams throughout your nursing program because it is critical that you know how to accurately calculate medication doses to help avoid medication errors. There are several ways to come to the correct answer. Use the method you were taught in your nursing program.

"Hot spots" may contain a diagram and a question that asks you to click on the part of the diagram that corresponds to your question. For example, you may be shown a diagram of a heart and asked to click on the spot that represents the most common congenital heart defect in children. In order to answer this, you would need to know that the most common defect is ventricular septal defect, and you would need to know where in the heart that defect is located (between the two ventricles).

The exam is comprehensive, so you may have a question about a depressed 80-year-old in heart failure, followed by one about a pregnant woman with diabetes mellitus, and then one about a six-year-old child with hemophilia and a sudden headache. As you may have noticed, the questions are integrated; each one tests your knowledge on more than one concept. Remember to carefully read the question but not "read into it." You need to answer the question on the computer screen, not the one you may be creating in your head.

Everything you need to know about NCLEX, including the NCLEX-PN and NCLEX-RN Test Plans and Candidate Bulletin can be found at: www.ncsb.org.

If you can graduate from a nursing program, you can pass NCLEX. Think positive—and prepare.

Preparing for the NCLEX Exam

Passing NCLEX is the rite of passage to your new career. Passing puts the RN or LPN after your name. Passing gives you the nursing salary you studied hard for. Not passing delays employment as a licensed nurse, creates loss of income, and can even result in low self-esteem. One study of nursing graduates who failed the NCLEX-RN showed several themes: carrying failure as a daily burden, losing their identity of being a nurse, doubting past accomplishments, seeing themselves as damaged goods, wanting support, and not daring to hope. These graduates said they felt cut off from the community of students and faculty who had been important to them while in their nursing program.

Passing NCLEX takes preparation that begins on your first day of your nursing program, so make sure to make use of the tips you learned in Chapter 3, as well as the suggestions noted here to help pass NCLEX. There is no magic formula for passing, and everyone has their own individual needs. Some nursing graduates need intensive preparation, while others need just a quick review. Most need something in between the two extremes.

1. Take ownership of your career. While others may help you, it ultimately remains up to you to pass NCLEX.
2. Plan to take the test as soon after graduation as possible, while all that information is still fresh in your mind. Studies show that early completion of NCLEX increases the chances of success; so the longer you wait the less likely it is that you will pass on your first try.
3. Focus. NCLEX focuses on safety, decision making, and prioritizing—much less than the fountain of knowledge you poured into your head throughout your nursing program. Therefore, this is the one time you want to focus on just what is on the test.

4. Study. NCLEX focuses on safety, decision making and prioritizing— not on everything you learned in school. Therefore, this is the one time you want to focus on just what is on the test. Whether you use self-study books, an online program, a live course, or the plan mandated by your nursing program, you need to brush up on content and test-taking skills. There is a cornucopia of available NCLEX-prep programs, most of which focus on the NCLEX-RN, so choose wisely. When in doubt, ask your nursing instructors for assistance in making the right choice for you. NLCEX-prep programs do add an extra cost to your nursing education costs; however, the price of failing NCLEX can be significantly higher. If you have financial difficulties, consider creating a NCLEX piggy bank when you begin your nursing education or asking for a NCLEX-prep program as a graduation gift.

   a. Self-study books: Several publishers and individual companies sell books designed to help you pass NCLEX. Be sure to choose one (or more) that is current (check the copyright date), include content, and have NCLEX style questions with rationales. Their questions should contain several alternative format questions for you to practice, as well as the rationales as to why the right answer is correct, and why all the other options are not.

   b. Online programs: These vary from strictly question-and-answer to programs with content video streaming. You may want to choose a comprehensive program that gives you content, questions with rationales, and test-taking skills, or, if you have not had much experience answering computerized questions, you may at least want to consider using a supplemental program that improves your ability to answer computerized questions.

   c. Live classes: Colleges and private companies offer NCLEX-prep courses that vary from 30 to 48 hours. When investigating a course, find out if: their faculty are experienced nurses or nurse educators; they include content, practice questions, and test-taking skills; and if they offer a refund or a free program should you not be successful taking the NCLEX exam.

5. Develop a study plan. Pull out your calendar and mark off the days until you take your exam, then schedule your study time. Don't be overly ambitious; be realistic, especially if you are going to work full-time

and/or care for a family, and don't cram in study right before the exam. Instead, plan to relax and revitalize the day before the exam.

6. Use your stress management skills. Eat right. Exercise regularly. Get adequate rest and sleep.

7. Manage your test anxiety by following steps 1 through 6 and step 8. You may also want to try deep breathing and other relaxation techniques, but if your test anxiety level has frequently interfered with your ability to pass previous exams, you may want to talk to your healthcare provider or your school counselor for a more individualized plan.

8. Maintain a positive attitude
   a. Post signs around your home and car that say, "I *will* pass NCLEX."
   b. Write your name with the letters LPN or RN after it.

Copy the sign below and fill in your name and appropriate title:

I will pass NCLEX

I	Initiate a study plan.
A	Avoid negative thoughts.
M	Maintain a positive attitude.
A	Answer lots of NCLEX-style questions.
N	No practice runs—pass on the first and only try.
U	Use appropriate study tools and guides.
R	Relax—manage your test anxiety.
S	Schedule your exam within a month after graduation.
E	Eat right, exercise, and get enough sleep.

_____   _____
(your name)   (RN or LPN)

Copyright © 2009 Mary Muscari

Taking the NCLEX Exam

Most nursing programs help you apply for licensure and the NCLEX exam because they care about their students and because they might lose their accreditation if they have continuously low pass rates. Besides offering assistance in test-taking skills, most help you with your licensure and NCLEX applications.

There are five steps and they are relatively simple:

Step 1. Go to the National Council of State Boards of Nursing (NCSBN) web site (www.ncsbn.org) and download and read their latest NCLEX Examination Candidate Bulletin.

Step 2. Submit your application for licensure board of nursing in the state where you plan to work. Make sure you meet all the state board requirements.

Step 3. Register and pay the fee for your NCLEX exam. You can register by mail, phone, or the Internet. The Pearson Vue NCLEX Exam website (www.vue.com/nclex) has further instructions for registration, as well as a search tool to look for test centers. (Tip: If you live in a small town, you may also use both your town and the nearest city for your search.)

Step 4. Schedule your exam. After you register and are made eligible, you will receive your Authorization to Test (ATT). You need this to schedule your exam and to be admitted to the exam center. When you schedule your exam, remember to plan for a testing session that may last a maximum of five (NCLEX-PN) or six (NCLEX-RN) hours. Don't delay scheduling. Some test centers fill up quickly, and your ATT has an expiration date. It's valid for a specific amount of time that is determined by your state board of nursing. You must schedule your NCLEX exam within that time, and the time frame cannot be extended under any circumstances. If you don't schedule when appropriate, you will have to reregister and pay another fee.

Step 5. Take your exam.

Getting Licensed in Another State

While the NCLEX exams are national, each state has its own licensure requirements. Therefore, you need to obtain licensure in your new state if you move. Begin by contacting the state board of nursing in your new state and asking them about their licensure requirements. Your new employer may also help you get your new license. You may need to take additional courses, but your new employer or state board of nursing can help you obtain those, too.

Once licensed in another state, you may opt to keep your original license. You can maintain licensure in multiple states as long as you continue to meet each state's requirements for license renewal.

The NCSBN has a program called the Nurse Licensure Compact (NLC) that allows nurses to have one license in their state of residency and to practice in other states, subject to each state's practice law and regulation. In order to practice across states under one license, you must legally reside in a NLC state to be eligible to have a multistate license. As of December 2008, participating states included: Arizona, Arkansas, Colorado, Delaware, Idaho, Iowa, Kentucky, Maine, Maryland, Mississippi, Nebraska, New Hampshire, New Mexico, North Carolina, North Dakota, Rhode Island, South Carolina, South Dakota, Tennessee, Texas, Utah, Virginia, and Wisconsin. If your state is not listed, check with your state board of nursing to see if has since joined NLC.

Renewing Your License

Most states require you to renew your nursing license every two to three years. Licensing boards usually send renewal notices prior to the expiration date of your license; however, failure to receive a renewal notice does not relieve you of the responsibility for renewing your license before the expiration date.

Renewal typically requires that you complete an application form and pay a fee. You will most likely again be asked about any criminal convictions and chemical dependencies that may have occurred since you were licensed, and you will also most likely be asked if there is or was any malpractice litigation against you. Many states now also require that you complete a minimum of mandatory continuing education hours to renew your license.

CONTINUING EDUCATION

The survival rate from childhood leukemia (acute lymphoblastic leukemia) has increased from less than 30 percent in 1970 to approximately 80 percent, and nurses now face the challenges of managing the long-term consequences faced by leukemia survivors. Healthcare continuously evolves. Therefore, nurses need to keep up-to-date with the changes. One of the ways to do this is with continuing education.

Continuing education is typically defined by state boards of nursing as "programs beyond the basic preparation that are designed to promote and enrich knowledge, improve skills, and develop attitudes for the enhancement of nursing practice, thus improving health care to the public." Several state boards of nursing mandate continuing education for license renewal, and other state boards of nursing plan to do this in the future.

Mandatory Continuing Education

Mandatory continuing education exists to require evidence that nurses maintain and update the nursing knowledge and skills needed to make competent decisions and judgments for nursing practice, education, administration, and/or research. As previous noted, many state boards of nursing require that nurses take mandatory courses to maintain their nursing license. Most of these boards specify a number of required hours, typically between 10 and 30, to be completed during each two- or three-year licensure cycle. Some require specific courses, such as medication error reduction, the Health Insurance Portability and Accountability Act (HIPAA), child abuse, elder abuse, HIV/AIDS, healthcare directives, bioterrorism, and end-of-life care. Some states have specific requirements for advanced practice nurses, especially in the area of pharmacology.

For those contract hours not specified, nurses are free to choose their own topics, as long as they pertain to nursing. Many nurses choose topics relevant to their specialty area, such as medical-surgical nursing, pediatrics, or women's health, while others choose role-specific topics, including administration and case management. Nurses may study practice related concepts, such as pharmacology, risk management, or legal issues. Nurses can also choose areas they wish to explore for a career change. For example, a critical care nurse may study community nursing to consider a career move to home health.

While you would have a wide variety of options to choose from to meet your state requirements, you still have to abide by your state's regulations. All insist that the continuing education courses relate to nursing practice, such as:

▶ direct patient care
▶ nursing specialty areas
▶ nursing management, supervision, and/or administration
▶ legal issues
▶ ethical issues
▶ nursing education
▶ quality management and improvement
▶ nursing theory
▶ nursing research
▶ therapeutic communications
▶ death and dying
▶ clinical technology and procedures

Most state boards of nursing approve continuing education activities sponsored by:

▶ approved professional nursing education programs
▶ accredited hospital and health care facilities
▶ national nursing, medical, osteopathic, and other health care professional organizations, as well as their state and regional affiliates
▶ federal and state agencies
▶ state boards of nursing in states other than the nurse's state of residency

Many states disallow certain types of courses, such as self-improvement, change in attitude, financial gain, courses designed for lay persons, BLS (Basic Life Support), mandatory annual education on facility-specific policies, and employment orientation programs. You may take these courses for your own satisfaction; however, you can't use them toward meeting your mandatory requirements.

Most states require nurses to maintain records of their continuing education courses for approximately five years. Nurses are not required to submit proof of their hours when they apply for license renewal; however, they are required to attest to the fact that they completed them. Nurses may be subject to disciplinary action if they wrongly claim to have completed the required continuing education, and states randomly select nurses for audits.

Nonmandatory Continuing Education

In those states where continuing education is not mandated, nurses may elect to take courses to enhance their careers or simply for self-improvement. You can even take personal enrichment courses designed for nurses: resume writing, surviving job conflict, and enhancing your creativity. While many states don't accept them for licensure, these courses can still enhance your career and be fun.

Where to Find Continuing Education Courses

Most nursing continuing education courses are just a mouse click away. A simple Google search can lead to pages of courses. You can take courses online as print courses, audio courses, podcasts, or webcasts; most require that you complete and pass a brief multiple choice quiz and a course evaluation to obtain credit. Online courses vary from 1 contact hour to 40. You can also obtain continuing education hours by attending approved conferences or taking college courses.

Continuing Education Lingo

Speaking of approvals and contact hours, continuing education has its own language. The following is a glossary of terms adapted from the American Nurses Association and the American Academy of Pediatrics.

accreditation. In-depth process by which an institution, organization, or agency is permitted to provide or approve quality continuing education over an extended period of time (usually one to three years).

accredited provider. Organization that is approved by the American Nurses Credentialing Center to provide quality continuing education over an extended period of time.

contact hour. Measurement unit that describes 60 minutes of an organized learning activity that is either a didactic or clinical experience.

continuing education unit (CEU). A standard measure of ten clock hours of educational activity used by many universities and professional organizations under the criteria of the International Association for Continuing Education and Training (IACET).

continuing medical education units (CMEs). Continuing educational activities for physicians and other health care professionals, accredited by the Accreditation Council for Continuing Medical Education (ACCME) to that CME activities meet accepted standards of education.

co-providership. The planning, developing, and implementing of an education activity by two or more organizations or agencies.

educational objective. Statement of learner outcome(s) that is measurable and achievable within a designated time frame.

evaluation. Process of determining quality through systematic appraisal and study.

learner directed. Activities initiated and implemented by the participant.

outcome. End result of any activity of the provider unit measured by written evaluation or change in practice.

provider. Individual, institution, organization, or agency responsible for the development, implementation, evaluation, financing, record keeping, and quality of nursing continuing education activities.

provider unit. The distinct body responsible for coordinating all aspects of the nursing continuing education activities.

CERTIFICATION AND CERTIFICATES

There are considerable differences between certification and certificates. Educational organizations and schools give certificates to indicate that a person completed a program, while certifying agencies certify an individual's mastery and competency via a set of standards. For example, a nurse can receive a certificate in complementary-alternative medicine (CAM) after completing an 11-hour continuing education course, but that does not indicate that the nurse has achieved a level of mastery in CAM.

The American Legal Nurse Consultant Certification Board (ALNCCB) certifies legal nurse consultants through their Legal Nurse Consultant Certified (LNCC) program. To meet their criteria for certification a person must be a licensed registered nurse who has practiced for at least five years, and who has evidence of completing 2,000 hours of legal nurse consulting experience in the last three years. Once this criteria is met, the nurse then successfully passes a certification exam. The ALNCCB clearly delineates between certification and certificate:

Certification versus Certificate

Certification

1. Results from a standardized assessment of a nurse's knowledge, skills, and competencies in a specific area
2. Usually requires professional experience
3. Awarded by a third party, usually a standard-setting organization and usually not for profit
4. Indicates mastery and competence according to set standards, usually via an application or examination
5. Standards set through a defensible, professionally recognized process that results in an outline of required knowledge and skills
6. Typically results in credentials to be used after name, such as LNCC (Legal Nurse Consultant Certified)
7. Has ongoing requirements to maintain certification or to recertify so that nurses show they continue to meet the requirements for certification

Certificate

1. Results from an educational activity
2. May be for novices or experienced nurses
3. Awarded by the educational organization that provides the educational activity; usually for profit
4. Indicates a course or series of courses other than a degree
5. Course content determined by providing agency or institution; usually not standardized
6. Usually results in a notation on one's resume
7. Nothing further occurs once course is completed and certificate is awarded

The American Nurses Credentialing Center (ANCC) is the largest nursing credentialing organization in the world. More than 75,000 advanced practice nurses are currently certified by the ANCC, which offers nursing certification in 26 different areas. The ANCC certifies nurses in their specialties or at advanced practice levels. Nurses can be ANCC certified in the following specialties: ambulatory care, cardiac rehabilitation, cardiovascular nursing, case management, college health, community health, geriatric nursing, high-risk perinatal (before/during/after birth) nursing, home health, informatics (technology), maternal-child nursing, medical-surgical nursing, nurse executive, nursing professional development, pain management, pediatric nursing, perinatal nursing, psychiatric mental-health nursing, and school nursing. ANCC certified advanced practice nurses are nurse practitioners, clinical specialists, or other specialists. ANCC certified nurses can renew their certification every six years through continuing education, academic credits, presentations, publications, and/or preceptorship, as well as the completion of 1,000 hours of clinical practice in their certification area, or they can retake and pass the certification exam.

There are other organizations that certify specific areas of nursing. The Pediatric Nursing Certification Board (www.pncb.org) has certification programs for pediatric nurses and primary care pediatric nurse practitioners, and the only certification program for acute care pediatric nurse practitioners. The American Midwifery Certification Board (www.amcbmidwife.org) certifies nurse midwives, and the Council on Certification of Nurse Anesthetists (www.aana.com) certifies nurse anesthetists. Sexual Assault Nurse Examiners can become certified through the International Association of Forensic Nurses. These organizations also have methods for maintaining or renewing certification.

NURSING NOTES

Nursing School Survival 101, by Monica Mazurowski

Preparing to get into nursing school: probably one of the most intimidating experiences of my life. Every school I applied to had a little * next to the nursing program and the statement "very limited space and difficult program." And at each open house I went to for the schools I heard something along the lines of "Look around, because only about 10 of the 40 students in this room will be accepted." However, I got into the four schools I applied to with good grades, Honor Society, some community service, and extracurriculars, but nothing over the top! I think being enthusiastic in your essay and being an all-around good student says more than a letter grade.

Admissions: I found this process to go relatively fast. I applied very early, probably in the first week you could apply, which I would also recommend doing, and heard back less than a month later from all the schools I applied to, either telling me I was accepted or that I had made it to the next round, so to speak.

Surviving Nursing School: Ah, the tough one. To be completely honest, I would consider myself a very balanced nursing student. I spent my first two years having a blast and managing As with all of my general education courses and then *boom*, junior year came along. My advice: Have fun while you're taking your easy classes! Once that third year rolled around, I went from waking up at 10:45 A.M. to make it to my 11 A.M. art class to waking up at 5:15 A.M. to be at clinical by 5:45. Talk about a drastic change!! Now don't get me wrong, nursing school is very challenging; however if you learn how to manage your time well you can still have a life. I work at a restuarant about 12 hours a week, have lots of friends and a serious boyfriend, and still manage to get As and Bs. For me, the key was to study a little bit each night. Then, the night before while everyone was cramming, okay, I was, too, but at least I wasn't going into the cramming blind! A lot of my peers were very intimidated by clinical and the stories we'd hear of evil clinical professors who made girls get sick every morning. That also is nothing to fear. If you simply come prepared, are confident in your answers, and genuinely want to learn, professors can see that, and though they will challenge you, they will also respect you. Another bit of advice I would give would be to not only do an internship after your junior year, but also to work as a nurse's aide the summer of your sophomore year. It will help you get your feet wet with your profession, gain essential skills, and have a heck of a lot more appreciation for those who are helping you when you become an RN.

CHAPTER six

NURSING AS A CAREER

WHEN NURSING is a job, you go to work and come home. When nursing is a career, you go a lot further. The difference is in the attitude. A career in nursing can take you along many different paths. There is a nursing specialty for every medical specialty, and more. If you know you want to be a nurse, begin to explore your options now so you can ask informed questions once you start your education. Research your special areas of interest and talk to faculty with similar interests to see if you can work with them on projects, such as research, clinical practice, or publications. Look into externships. These give you insight on the specialty and resume material to help you get a position in that specialty.

You should have no difficulty finding a nursing job given the shortage. But don't settle. Look for the job you want. Plan ahead. You'll be a lot less stressed if you know you have a job waiting for you when you graduate. Look into the best nursing positions (Appendix B), and use the national and state nurses associations (Appendix C) for their career development features. Create a great resume and learn how to interview for that perfect job.

NURSING SPECIALTIES

Nursing has come a long way from the days when caring for the sick in hospitals was seen as the sole nursing role. While nurses still care for ill clients, many of these clients are in the community or at home. Nurses also focus on wellness and health maintenance, as well as the psychological, cognitive, social, and spiritual needs of clients.

Many of the nursing specialties described here require that you be a registered nurse, and some require additional training. But these requirements may vary per institution, so if a hospital or outpatient center has your special area of interest and you are a practical nurse, ask them about the requirements before you rule them out. Many specialties have available certifications. Most of these certifications require that you have experience, continuing education in the specialty, and a certification exam.

Ambulatory Care Nursing

American Academy of Ambulatory Care Nurses: www.aaacn.org

Ambulatory care nursing is characterized by rapid, focused assessments of patients, long-term nurse/patient/family relationships, and teaching and translating prescriptions for care into doable activities for patients and their caregivers. The emphasis is on pain management and client education to keep people with injuries and chronic injuries healthy and independent in their home surroundings. Ambulatory care nurses respond rapidly to high volumes of patients in a short period of time and deal with issues that are not always predictable. Ambulatory care nurses work in community-based hospitals, schools, workplaces, and homes. Client encounters may be face-to-face, via phone, or via another communication device.

Camp Nursing

Association of Camp Nurses: www.campnurse.org

Camp nurses work in traditional camps or camps for children with disabilities or chronic illnesses, either of which may be day camp or residential. They provide routine and emergency care to children and staff, monitor children with chronic diseases, educate campers and staff on prevention, and collaborate with camp administrators to develop and implement policies that reduce the risk of injury or illness. Flexibility, critical thinking skills, and problem solving skills enable camp nurses to protect and promote the health of the entire camp community. Humor and creativity help, too. Camp nurses deal with problems as simple as lice and as complex as diabetes or HIV/AIDS. They review health records, assess, administer medications, dress wounds, calm separation anxiety, and manage behavioral problems. Camp nurses also attend to the needs of staff, who may present with illnesses, infections, or injuries.

Cardiac Rehabilitation Nursing

Association of Rehabilitation Nurses: www.rehabnurse.org

Cardiac rehabilitation nurses provide assessment, support, and education for clients with heart disease who need to make lifestyle changes to prevent their disease from getting worse. They work in hospitals, ambulatory care, and fitness centers, and their clients include people recovering from heart attacks or heart surgery. Cardiac rehabilitation nurses monitor these clients during exercise to prevent injury and overexertion, promote stress management, and teach healthy diet, adequate exercise, and smoking cessation. ANCC provides certification as a cardiac rehabilitation nurse.

Case Management Nursing

Case Management Society of America: www.cmsa.org

Case management nurses organize and coordinate individualized resources and services for clients. They work with clients of all ages, with all types of illnesses and health problems and in all types of healthcare settings, but many target specific populations, such as older adults or people post organ transplant. The case manager's goal is to foster quality self-care. Case managers use a plan of care called *clinical pathway* to assess the needs and progress of their clients. ANCC offers certification for nurses as case managers.

College Health Nurse

American College Health Association: www.acha.org

College health nurses work in college health centers to assist students with health maintenance, illness prevention, and illness management. They also maintain health records and assure that immunizations and other wellness needs are up-to-date. Since most students are young adults, college health nurses focus on issues such as dating safety, sexually transmitted disease prevention, and sports injury prevention. However, as more adults return to college, college health nurses face new challenges, such as the prevention of cardiovascular problems. Most illnesses and injuries are minor, like sore throats and sprained ankles, but college nurses still need to be ready for emergencies, including ones related to psychiatric disorders. ANCC provides certification for college health nurses.

Community Health Nurses

Association of Community Health Nurse Educators: www.achne.org

Community health nurses work in the field through government and private agencies. They work with individuals, families, and groups to improve their overall health by educating them about common issues such as illness prevention, parenting, elder care, and healthcare problems, as well as issues pertinent to that community such as lead poisoning and farm safety. Community health nurses provide home follow-up care, immunization clinics, health education, and referral of clients to appropriate agencies for assistance. Community health nurses need to be well versed in disaster management including sudden mass casualty incidents, unfolding infectious disease outbreaks, or evolving environmental disaster. While bioterrorism is always a concern, flooding is more commonplace and often just as deadly. ANCC offers certification for community health nurses.

Correctional Health Nursing

American Correctional Health Organization: www.achsa.org

National Commission on Correctional Health Care: www.ncchc.org

Correctional health nursing provides freedom of practice in a restricted environment—jails and prisons. Correctional nurses remain neutral and unbiased by their clients' offenses and assure that their clients receive the same healthcare treatment they would receive if not incarcerated. One of the key issues in correctional health is the issue of custody versus care. Correctional nurses provide quality care within the necessity of custody because safety comes first. Correctional nurses care for their clients from intake until release and must be proficient in assessment, infectious diseases, responding to emergencies, the needs of an aging prison population, and managing chronic illnesses and psychiatric disorders. They also need to differentiate legitimate complaints from malingering in clients who can be very manipulative. There are a number of opportunities for growth in the corrections field, with roles ranging from staff nurse to manager to nurse practitioner to director. Nursing does not offer certification in correctional health; however the National Commission on Correctional Health Care (NCCHC) offers basic and advanced certification in correctional health care called the Certified Correctional Health Professional (CCHP).

Critical Care Nursing

American Association of Critical-Care Nurses: www.aacn.org

Critical care nurses work with clients who have life-threatening conditions due to illness, injury, or major surgery. They provide complex assessment, high-intensity interventions, and continuous nursing care. Critical care nurses require a specialized body of knowledge, experience, and skills to provide care to patients and their families. Critical care nurses work in a variety of intensive care units: cardiac, burn, medical, surgical, neurological, neonatal, and pediatric. The American Association of Critical-Care Nurses provides certification programs for the following subspecialties: adult, neonatal, pediatric, progressive care, cardiac medicine, cardiac surgery, and nurse manager and leader.

Developmental Disabilities Nursing

Developmental Disabilities Nursing Association: www.ddna.org

Developmental disabilities nurses work with clients who have developmental disabilities, including mental retardation and autistic spectrum disorders. These clients range in age from infant to older adult and many have associated problems such as cerebral palsy, hearing and/or visual impairment, and seizure disorders. Developmental disability nurses provide holistic care, meeting the client and family's physical, cognitive, emotional, social, and spiritual needs. The Developmental Disabilities Nursing Association provides a certification program for developmental disabilities nurses.

Emergency Nursing

Emergency Nurses Association: www.ena.org

Emergency nursing crosses all ages and areas of nursing to provide care that include birth, death, injury prevention, women's health, disease, and life and limb saving measures. Emergency nurses apply the nursing process to clients of all ages requiring stabilization and/or resuscitation for a variety of illnesses and injuries. Emergency nurses work in hospital emergency departments; military settings; clinics, health maintenance organizations, and ambulatory care centers; business, educational, industrial, and correctional institutions; and other healthcare environments. Emergency care also happens at the point of contact, where clients live, work, play, and go to school. The Emergency Nurses Association provides certification for emergency nurses, pediatric emergency nurses, and ground transportation nurses.

Flight Nursing

Air and Surface Transport Nurses Association: www.astna.org

Flight nurses care for emergent and nonemergent clients during surface and air transportation, including interfacility transport and emergency scene calls for medical emergencies and trauma. Cases range from the simple to the challenging. Prerequisites to becoming a flight nurse include three to five years of critical care nursing, Advanced Cardiac Life Support (ACLS) certification, and usually Pediatric Advanced Life Support (PALS) certification. Flight nurses are employed by trauma centers and other acute care facilities, public and private transport companies, and the military. The Air and Surface Transport Nurses Association (ASTNA) provides certification as either a certified flight registered nurse or certified transport registered nurse. The Board of Certification of the Emergency Nurses Association also provides certification for flight nurses.

Forensic Nursing

International Association of Forensic Nurses: www.iafn.org

Now more than ever, healthcare frequently becomes enmeshed with the legal system, creating numerous opportunities for healthcare providers in the field of forensic health. The word *forensic* means "pertaining to the law." Forensic nursing applies to those instances where nurses interact with the law or legal issues. Forensic nursing is the application of nursing science to public or legal proceedings, the application of the forensic aspects of nursing in the scientific investigation and treatment of trauma and/or death of victims and perpetrators of abuse, violence, criminal activity, traumatic accidents, and environmental hazards. Forensic nurses work in a number of settings with a variety of clients: sexual assault victims and perpetrators; victims and perpetrators of domestic violence, child abuse, and elder abuse; juvenile delinquents; victims of traumatic accidents; clients with criminal backgrounds; and mentally disturbed offenders. Forensic nurses can also: work in the coroner's office on death investigations; assist law enforcement in collecting evidence; act as legal consultants; work with medical malpractice issues; work in organ and tissue donation; deal with environmental issues (food and drug tampering, hazards, terrorism, epidemiological issues); and create violence prevention programs. Healthcare settings that deal with forensic issues include, but are not limited to: emergency treatment facilities, schools, correctional facilities, psychiatric settings, and outpatient and community health settings. Forensic health research is a rapidly growing area.

Gastroenterology/Endoscopy Nursing

Society of Gastroenterology Nurses and Associates: www.sgna.org

American Board of Certification for Gastroenterology Nurses: http://www.abcgn.org/

Gastroenterology/endoscopy nurses provide essential care to clients undergoing screening, diagnostic, and treatment procedures for gastrointestinal problems. Some of these nurses specialize in endoscopy, the use of a flexible scope to examine the gastrointestinal tract. Gastroenterology nurses work in hospitals, outpatient centers, and private offices. The American Board of Certification for Gastroenterology Nurses and the Society of Gastroenterology Nurses and Associates offer certification for gastroenterology nurses.

Genetic Nursing

International Society of Nurses in Genetics: www.isong.org

Genetic Nurses Credentialing Commission: www.geneticnurse.org

Genetic nurses work with clients of all ages who have, or who are suspected of having, a genetic disease or disorder, such as cystic fibrosis, neuromuscular disease, and Down Syndrome. Genetic nurses work with other healthcare specialists to provide risk identification, screening, diagnostic testing, and treatment. They work as case managers, program coordinators, genetic counselors, and educators at university medical centers and research facilities. The psychosocial impact of having a child with a possibly incurable genetic disease or disorder can be traumatic, thus genetic nurses also need psychosocial skills to support and assist families in handling these conditions. The Genetic Nurses Credentialing Commission offers certification for genetic nurses.

Gerontological Nursing

National Gerontological Nursing Association: www.ngna.org

Gerontological nurses care for the physical and psychological needs of older adults in a variety of settings, including hospitals, long-term care facilities, community health centers, senior centers, and client homes. They focus on maximizing clients' functional abilities, as well as promoting, maintaining, and restoring health. ANCC offers certification for gerontological nurses.

HIV/AIDS Nursing

HIV/AIDS Nursing Certification Board: www.hancb.org/about.htm

HIV/AIDS nurses provide educational, therapeutic, and supportive interventions. Their goals are to prevent infection; promote client, family, and community adaptation to HIV infection and its sequelae; and to ensure continuity of client care by collaborating with the interdisciplinary team. HIV/AIDS nursing requires knowledge and skills that include pathophysiology, learning principles, family dynamics, grief and loss, coping with chronic illness, care of immunocompromised clients, risk assessment, and risk reduction. HIV/AIDS nurses use research findings to maintain an adequate knowledge base in an evolving field such as HIV/AIDS nursing. Care is multifocused and occurs in an array of settings including primary care, acute care institutions, communities, and schools. The HIV/AIDS Nursing Certification Board offers certification for HIV/AIDS nurses.

Holistic Nurses

American Holistic Nurses Association: www.ahna.org

American Holistic Nurses Credentialing Corporation: www.ahncc.org/pages/1/index.htm

Holistic nurses use the mind-body-spirit-emotion approach to the practice of nursing. They act as a bridge between conventional healthcare and complementary alternative health care since they are educated in both models. Complementary alternative health refers to health practices that incorporate plant, animal, and mineral-based medicines, spiritual therapies, manual techniques, and exercises. Holistic nurses work in a number of settings and may specialize in one or more modalities, such as aromatherapy or energetic healing. The American Holistic Nurses Credentialing Corporation provides certification for holistic nurses.

Home Health Nurses

Home Healthcare Nursing Association: www.hhna.org

Visiting Nurse Association of American: www.vnaa.org

A specific type of community health nurse, home health nurses, also called visiting nurses, provide cost-effective and compassionate home healthcare to some of the nation's most vulnerable individuals, particularly the elderly and individuals with disabilities. They enable these persons to meet their healthcare needs at home and avoid expensive hospitalization. ANCC offers certification for home health nurses.

Hospice and Palliative Care Nursing

Hospice and Palliative Care Nurses Association: www.hpna.org

National Board for the Certification of Hospice and Palliative Care Nurses: www.nbchpn.org

Hospice and palliative care nurses aim to relieve suffering and improve the quality of life for persons who are living with, or dying from, advanced illness, as well as those who are bereaved. Hospice care can take place at a hospice or at home, as it is a philosophy and not a location. Hospice and palliative care nurses aim to relieve suffering, control symptoms, and restore functional capacity, while remaining sensitive to personal, cultural, and religious values, beliefs and practices. Hospice and palliative care nurses work in collaboration with the interdisciplinary team but distinguish themselves from their colleagues in other nursing specialty practices by their unwavering focus on end-of-life care.

Infection Control Nurses

Association for Professionals in Infection Control and Epidemiology: www.apic.org

Certification Board of Infection Control and Epidemiology: www.cbic.org

Nurses play a critical role in preventing and controlling infectious disease, including tuberculosis, HIV/AIDS, and nosocomial (developed in hospital) infections. Infection control nurses identify, control, and prevent outbreaks of infections in hospitals, long-term care facilities, and community agencies. Infection control nurses collect and analyze infection control data; plan, implement, and evaluate infection prevention and control measures; educate individuals about infection risk, prevention, and control; develop and revise infection control policies and procedures; investigate suspected outbreaks of infection; and provide consultation on infection risk assessment, prevention, and control strategies. The Certification Board of Infection Control and Epidemiology, Inc. (CBIC) is a voluntary autonomous multidisciplinary board that provides direction for and administers the certification process for professionals in infection control and applied epidemiology.

Informatics Nursing

American Informatic Nursing Association: www.ania.org

Nursing informatics integrates nursing science, computer science, and information science to manage and communicate data, information, and knowledge in nursing practice. Informatics involves all aspects of computerization as it relates to nursing and healthcare, but informatic nurses may specialize in certain areas. This fast growing field is used in hospitals, computer hardware/software companies, health care consulting firms, educational institutions, regulatory agencies, and pharmaceutical and research facilities. ANCC offers certification for informatic nurses.

Intravenous Therapy Nurse

Infusion Nurses Society: www.ins1.org

Infusion Nurses Certification Corporation: http://incc1.i4a.com

Intravenous (IV) therapy nurses initiate, monitor, and terminate therapies including medications, antineoplastic agents, investigational drugs, blood products, and parenteral nutrition. They performs venous and arterial punctures, maintain the intravascular site including tubing and dressings, monitor for infections, and assess patients for adverse reactions and complications. The Infusion Nurses Certification Corporation provides certification for infusion nurses.

Lactation Consultant

International Lactation Consultant Association: www.ilca.org/examprep.html

International Board of Lactation Consultant Examiners: www.iblce.org

Lactation consultant nurses help new mothers master breast-feeding and manage problems that may arise. Lactation consultant nurses advocate for breast-feeding mothers in the workplace, and they work in the health policy arena to encourage the development of progressive breast-feeding programs and legislation.

Legal Nurse Consultants

American Association of Legal Nurse Consultants: www.aalnc.org

A group of forensic nurses, legal nurse consultants (LNCs) act as legal consultants on medical issues, particularly lawsuits. Other LNCs work with product liability, child custody, elder law, or criminal cases. LNCs work with law firms on cases to review medical records and client treatment. Some work as salaried employees, others independently. LNCs can educate attorneys about standards of medical care; explain medical procedures; and provide assistance with discovery requests, deposition questions, and the selection of expert witnesses. The American Association of Legal Nurse Consultants offers certification to legal nurse consultants.

Medical-Surgical Nursing (Adult Health Nursing)

Academy of Medical Surgical Nurses: www.medsurgnurse.org

The foundation for nursing practice, medical-surgical nursing has evolved from an entry-level position to an adult health specialty. Medical-surgical nurses care for adult patients in many settings, such as hospitals, clinics, ambulatory care units, home healthcare, long-term care, urgent care centers, and surgical centers. Medical-surgical nurses perform assessments, and administer care, treatments, and medications. ANCC provides certification for medical-surgical nurses.

NURSING NOTES

Never Forgotten, by Tina Abbate

I still vividly recall my first few days in the neonatal intensive care unit. I was a new graduate, a fresh-faced registered nurse, ready to conquer the world. My desire to vanquish quickly vanished (as did the color from my face) as I took my first steps onto the unit and surveyed my surroundings. Alarms beeped and blared haphazardly while people scurried around, exuding an aura of importance and purpose. Individuals garbed in stark white coats were huddled together at a bedside with brows wrinkled and engaged in an apparently intellectual discourse. I captured blips of important conversations: "the TPN was lowered to 5cc/hr," "the doctor wants an ABG at 10 o'clock."

TPN? ABG? What could that possibly mean? Is everything an acronym around here?

I felt like the lone duck in a gaggle of geese.

I met baby Alex [pseudonym] on the second day of my orientation. He was two hours old, tipping the scale at 430 grams. It seemed implausible for a baby weighing less than a pound to survive outside of the womb. He was born prematurely by nearly four months. His head was barely the size of a baseball and his body was practically devoid of the vital protective layer of fat. His eyes were fused shut. His skin was translucent and rather gelatinous looking. Baby Alex could fit into the palms of your hands.

I had never seen a baby that small up close and frankly, I could not stop staring. All of the technology that surrounded him—a ventilator, IV pumps, a radiant warmer—catapulted me into an entranced state. These machines represented Alex's life support. These machines gave compromised neonates a fighting chance at survival. We had a lot to do for our pint-sized patient. His response to the ventilator was less than desirable. The doctors made numerous adjustments, slowly increasing the pressure necessary to expand his stiff, underdeveloped lungs. Blood work, paperwork, vital signs, IV fluids, suctioning—how will I ever make sense of it all?

Alex's mom and dad came into the NICU around noon to visit their son for the first time. They sat quietly at his bedside for quite some time and finally Mom turned to me and asked, "Is he going to die?" How could I possibly answer her appropriately? I fumbled around in my head, desperately trying to think of the appropriate response. Another nurse quickly said, "Alex is very sick, and we are trying everything within our power to help him live."

Twelve hours had passed and my shift was over. Alex was 14 hours old and actually demonstrated signs of improvement. He finally responded to the vent, as indicated by his blood work. A glimmer of hope sparkled for the first time. I sent Alex a mental message, "Hang in there, little man. I will see you tomorrow."

The next day arrived and I marched into the NICU, chin up, and ready to face the challenges that loomed ahead. I walked into Alex's room and went toward the back wall where he was stationed yesterday. He was not there. I assumed that the night nurses moved him to another room. I approached a night shift nurse, "What room did they move Alex to?" She smiled apologetically. "Alex died this morning, around 3:00."

It felt as if someone had forcibly kicked me in the chest. I hurried away and ran to the nearest bathroom. I sobbed uncontrollably. I asked, "Why, darn it why?" With all of the modern medical ministrations we have readily available, Alex should still be alive.

Babies represent a beautiful futuristic hope. Some grow up to become influential pillars of our society and some die before they even have the chance. In a threefold utopian dream, all babies would be healthy and robust, leading full lives, devoid of any pain or suffering. Reality, unfortunately, dictates a different story.

I embarked on two startling realizations. First, it is okay to submit to your emotions. Second, the nurse's involvement within the family dynamic is far more considerable than I had ever imagined. As nurses, we are inherently embedded within the fabric of a patient's story. It is okay to thrust your heart and soul into your profession and there is no harm or shame in displaying natural emotions. I would imagine that suppression of these raw sentiments might progress into impairment for the long term. After all, we are humans caring for humans.

Dr. John De Frain stated, in the early 1990s, "The death of a baby is like a stone cast into the stillness of a quiet pool; the concentric ripples of despair sweep out in all directions, affecting many, many people." We will never forget baby Alex.

Neonatal Nursing

Academy of Neonatal Nursing: www.academyonline.org

National Association for Neonatal Nurses: www.nann.org

Neonatal nurses work in a Level I (healthy newborn), II (intermediate care), or III (intensive care) nursery. Neonatal nurses perform the initial bath and nursing assessment on newborns and provide continuous care for them in the nursery. They teach new mothers basic baby care, as well as safety, including safe sleep practices and shaken baby syndrome. Neonatal intensive care nurses can pursue credentialing through the Emergency Nurses Association, as noted in the emergency nursing section.

Occupational Health Nursing

American Association of Occupational Health Nurses: www.aaohn.org

American Board of Occupational Nursing: www.abohn.org

Occupational and environmental health nurses deliver health and safety programs and services to workers and community groups. Their practice focuses on health promotion and restoration, prevention of illness and injury, and protection from work-related and environmental hazards. Occupational and environmental health nurses blend business knowledge with healthcare expertise to balance the requirement for a safe and healthful work environment. Occupational and environmental health nurses work in a variety of employee health centers, providing case management, counseling and crisis management, and health promotion and risk reduction. They deal with legal and regulatory compliance issues, as well as worker and workplace hazard detection. The American Board of Occupational Nursing offers certification as occupational health nurses, occupational health case managers, or occupational health nurse safety.

Oncology Nursing

Oncology Nursing Society: www.ons.org

Oncology Nursing Certification Corporation: www.oncc.org

Oncology nurses work with clients who have cancer, those at risk for cancer, and those who survive cancer. Oncology nursing encompasses the roles of direct caregiver, educator, consultant, administrator, and researcher, and oncology nurses work in all care settings where clients experiencing or at risk for developing cancer receive care, education, and counseling for cancer prevention, screening, and detection. Oncology nurses also function as coordinators of care, collaborating with other cancer care providers and team members to provide required care as effectively as possible. The Oncology Nursing Certification Corporation provides certification for oncology nurses.

Orthopedic Nursing

National Association of Orthopedic Nurses: www.orthonurse.org

Orthopedic Nurses Certification Board: www.oncb.org

Orthopedic nursing spans the entire continuum of care from birth until death, illness to prevention, acute to rehab to care in patients' homes. Nurses who care for patients with musculoskeletal injuries and conditions need to have the appropriate knowledge and skills specific to the orthopedic specialty.

Parish Nursing

National Health Ministries: www.pcusa.org/nationalhealth/parishnursing

Parish nurses serve members of their congregation and often people in the community as well. Parish nurses: promote healthy lifestyles and help people understand the relationships between lifestyle, faith, and well-being; help people sort out health problems and make appropriate plans for handling them; act as a communication link and support for community health resources and services, to provide referrals and be a liaison for the church and its members; recruit volunteers and train them to carry out a range of supportive services; assist groups in the congregation with particular concerns: and assist with the assessment of congregational and community health needs. Most parish nurses perform this role as volunteers.

Perioperative Nursing

American Association of periOperative Nursing:www.aorn.org

Competency & Credentialing Institute: www.cc-institute.org

Perioperative nurses assess, plan, and implement the nursing care patients receive before, during, and after surgery. They perform client assessment, create and maintain a sterile and safe surgical environment, provide pre- and post-operative patient education, monitor the patient's physical and emotional well-being, and integrate and coordinate patient care throughout the surgical care continuum.

Perioperative nurses may assume one of the following roles during surgery:

► Scrub nurses work directly with the surgeon within the sterile field by passing instruments, sponges, and other items needed during the procedure.

► Circulating nurses work outside the sterile field and manage the nursing care within the operating room by assisting the surgery team in creating and maintaining a safe, comfortable environment.

► RN first assistants deliver direct surgical care and may directly assist the surgeon by controlling bleeding and by providing wound exposure and suturing during the actual procedure (requires additional education).

Perioperative nurses may become O.R. directors, managing budgets, staffing, and other business aspects of the operating room.

Perinatal Nursing

National Association of Neonatal Nurses: www.nann.org

Perinatal nurses care for women, newborns, and their families from the beginning of pregnancy through the first month of the newborn's life (perinatal period). They assess the progression of labor, monitor the status of the baby and mother, maintain the mother's comfort, support the family, foster the maternal-child bond, teach parenting skills, assesses and support the mother in her recovery from childbirth, and evaluate the newborn's adjustment to life. ANCC provides certification for perinatal nurses.

Psychiatric Mental Health Nursing

American Psychiatric Nurses Association: www.apna.org

International Association of Psychiatric Nurses: www.ispn-psych.org

Psychiatric mental-health nurses work with individuals, families, groups, and communities to assess mental health needs, develop diagnoses, and plan, implement, and evaluate nursing care. They promote and foster mental health, assess dysfunction, and assist clients to regain or improve their coping abilities and prevent further disability. These interventions focus on psychiatric mental-health clients and include health promotion, development and maintenance of a therapeutic environment; assisting clients with self-care activities; administering and monitoring psychobiological treatment regimens; mental health teaching, including psychoeducation; crisis intervention and counseling, and case management. ANCC offers certification for psychiatric mental-health nurses.

Radiologic and Imaging Nursing

Association for Radiologic and Imaging Nursing: www.arinursing.org

Radiologic and imaging nurses practice in diagnostic and interventional radiology and imagery, such as ultrasonography, computerized tomography, nuclear medicine, magnetic resonance, radiation oncology, and cardiac catheterization. Advances in medical technology and higher levels of care needed for an increasingly sicker patient population have made this area of nursing more challenging, but also in more demand. Radiologic and imaging nurses require critical care skills for those patients who may decompensate during the procedure and good psychiatric skills to manage client anxiety related to the equipment. The Association for Radiologic and Imaging Nursing offers certification for radiologic and imaging nurses.

Rehabilitation Nurses

Association of Rehabilitation Nurses: www.rehabnurse.org

Rehabilitation Nursing Certification Board: www.rehabnurse.org/pdf/alternate.pdf

Rehabilitation nurses provide care to people of all ages in order to facilitate recovery of functional abilities, prevent complications, and restore optimal wellness. They provide comprehensive rehabilitative care to patients with a broad spectrum of medical diagnoses and acuity in a collaborative, interdisciplinary, healthcare model. Rehabilitation nursing skills include transfer skills, application of splints and devices, eating techniques, memory improvement, fall prevention, continence training, behavior management, and crisis prevention and management. The Rehabilitation Nursing Certification Board offers certification for rehabilitation nurses.

School Nurse

National Association of School Nurses: www.nasn.org

National Board for Certification of School Nurses: www.nbcsn.com

School nurses support student learning by implementing strategies that promote student and staff health and safety. School nurses: screen for health problems, serve as the coordinator of the health services program, and provide nursing care; provide health education to students, staff, and parents; identify health and safety concerns in the school environment and promote a nurturing social environment; support healthy food services programs; promote healthy physical education, sports policies, and practices; provide health counseling, assess mental health needs, provide interventions, and refer students to appropriate school staff or community agencies; promote community involvement in assuring a healthy school; serve as school liaison to a health advisory committee; provide health education and counseling; and promote healthy activities and environment for school staff. School nurses work with children with special needs and perform pediatric nursing procedures such as gastrostomy tube feedings, tracheostomy care, and catheterization; screening for health factors impacting student learning; activities to promote health and prevent teen pregnancy, sexually transmitted diseases, tobacco, alcohol, and substance use and abuse; chronic disease management and education, administering medications; crisis team participation; recommending health curricula and guidelines for school district health policies; and serving as a healthcare provider liaison between the school and community. The National Board for Certification of School Nurses and the ANCC offer certification for school nurses.

Sexual Assault Nurse Examiner (SANE)

Sexual Assault Nurse Examiner/Sexual Assault Response Team: www.sane-sart.com

International Association of Forensic Nurses: www.iafn.org

Sexual assault nurse examiners (SANEs) are registered nurses who have been specifically trained to provide comprehensive care to sexual violence victims. SANEs are trained to identify physical trauma, document injuries, collect evidence, and maintain the chain of custody, testify, and provide necessary referrals. Registered nurses must successfully complete a 40-hour training and an additional 40 to 60 hours of supervised clinical experience to become SANEs. Certification for SANEs is available through the International Association of Forensic Nurses.

Telenursing

International Society for Telemedicine and eHealth: www.isft.net/cms/index.php?telenursing

Telenursing is the practice of nursing over distance using telecommunications technology. The nurse practices nursing by interacting with clients at a remote site to electronically receive the clients' health status data, initiate and transmit therapeutic interventions and regimens, and monitor and record clients' response and nursing care outcomes. The value of telenursing to the client is increased access to skilled, empathetic, and effective nursing delivered by means of telecommunications technology.

Transplant Nursing

International Transplant Nursing Society: http://itns.org

American Board for Transplant Certification: www.abtc.net

Transplant nurses care for transplant recipient and living donor clients throughout the transplantation process from end-stage disease through intraoperative experience to aftercare and follow-up. Transplant nurses need to possess a strong knowledge base of ethics, cultural implications, and legal issues related to transplants. The American Board for Transplant Certification offers certification for transplant nurses.

Trauma Nurses

Society of Trauma Nurses: www.traumanurses.org

Trauma nurses respond quickly to a wide variety of single- and multisystem traumatic situations involving different patient needs, ages, cultures, and severity of presenting symptoms. Trauma nurses must respond with decisiveness and clarity to unexpected events by assessing, intervening, and stabilizing patients about whom there is minimal information. Trauma nurses typically work in critical care or transport units and may seek certification as critical care nurses.

Women's Health Nursing

Association of Women's Health, Obstetric and Neonatal Nurses: www.awhonn.org/awhonn

Formerly called obstetrical-gynecological nursing, this specialty focuses on all of women's health, particularly the childbearing and reproductive health needs of women. Women's health nurses work with women during the prenatal, natal, and postnatal experiences and with women with gynecological problems, such as ovarian cancer. They also teach reproductive wellness, such as menopause management.

Wound, Ostomy and Continence Nursing

Wound, Ostomy and Continence Nurses Society: www.wocn.org

Wound, Ostomy and Continence Nurses Certification Board: www.wocncb.org

Wound, ostomy, and continence nurses provide support and evidence-based nursing care for individuals with urinary or fecal stomas, vascular and pressure wounds, draining wounds, neuropathic wounds, and fistulas. They also work with clients with bowel or bladder continence issues, and help all these clients manage their conditions. The Wound, Ostomy and Continence Nurses Certification Board offers certification to wound, ostomy, and continence nurses.

NURSING NOTES

Finding My Niche, by Jessica Schmoyer

Niche. It's such a simple word we all learn back in grammar school, just another word to add into our vocabulary bank. After the end of my third year of nursing school, I had yet to find mine. Tears flowed on occasion, while I wondered, *Did I pick the right major? Did I waste three years of college tuition for nothing?* My mother continually reassured me, saying I still had my externship in the summer and that I also had a complete year of school left. She knew me well enough, and she knew exactly what I would love.

During my summer externship I was placed into the Emergency Department (ED) for two weeks. While I was with my nurse preceptor a loud page came over the loud-speaker, "Trauma Alert. ETA 5 minutes." My nurse quickly shooed me away from our less acutely ill patients to go see the trauma team work their magic. A 19-year-old man had been brought in by med-evac after falling 60 feet from a tree. Each person in the trauma bay worked quickly, as one whole unit, each knowing their different role. He was in critical shape, and I watched as they placed a chest tube, established he had a broken femur and numerous facial fractures, and had lost all but two of his teeth. It was a gruesome sight, but I fell in love with it.

On another occasion I was able to jump on an experience to fly along with a different med-evac team. Since it was snowing in the morning, the flight team was able to show me around and teach me the tricks of the trade for safely operating within and around a helicopter. As the day went on and we had to turn down more and more flights because of the weather I became disheartened, afraid that I had driven two and a half hours and wouldn't get an opportunity to fly. Fortunately a break in the snow came, and we flew. We were able to fly to the scene of a car crash with an elderly woman. The paramedics and flight nurses worked fast, establishing a history, starting IVs, and administering medications. Once again, I was hooked. My heart was pounding from excitement. This had definitely become more than worth the tank of gas I had used that day.

As a nursing student, finding your niche can be tough. The paperwork can easily seem to drag down the real experiences you can gain in clinicals. Get out there: volunteer, shadow, ask nurses at clinical if they have anything interesting going on. Experience is the only way you'll figure out what you love, and once you find what you love, do everything you can to get there. From day one of nursing school my mother knew I would fall in love with trauma and the everyday hectic world of the ED. I found out by gaining experience outside of the clinical realm.

FINDING YOUR NICHE IN NURSING

Some people enter their nursing program knowing their chosen career path, be it pediatrics, critical care, or psychiatric nursing. Most people, however, are unsure. Don't be concerned if you have no idea about what type of nursing career will work best for you. You'll figure it out when you're in school going through your clinical rotations, or you'll have a defining moment that you can help create. Encourage your student nurses association to bring in nurses from different specialties to do panel presentations. Talk to your instructors and ask them about their career history. Find out how they started and how their career path led to teaching. Many instructors practice; ask if you can shadow them for a day or two. Read, read, and read. Journal articles provide as much insight on careers as they do on nursing care.

To increase your chances of obtaining a job in your specialty area, get some experience before you graduate. Nursing clinical rotations are pretty standard. All have adult health (medical-surgical nursing), pediatrics, and women's health; most have psychiatric nursing; and BSN programs have community health and critical care. Some programs offer nursing specialty electives, especially perioperative nursing, disaster nursing, and holistic nursing. These electives may or may not have practicum experience, but every little bit helps. A didactic course in palliative care still makes you a more desirable employee than another graduate with no palliative care background. If your program offers your specialty of interest, take it. If not, get creative:

- ▶ If your program has options for independent study, ask to use it to get experience in the specialty that interests you.
- ▶ Do a Web search to see if another school offers an elective course in your specialty. Many universities offer these courses online. Just make sure the credits will transfer if you need them to graduate.
- ▶ Volunteer. If you want to work in pediatrics, volunteer at a day care center; if you want to work in palliative care, volunteer at a hospice.
- ▶ Work with faculty on their research projects or publications.
- ▶ Write your own articles. As a student, you already have enough knowledge to write a case study.

Every little bit helps because the bits become resume material. Nurse recruiters will see you as someone willing to do more than only what's needed to get by, and you will be a better nurse because you'll have more knowledge.

JOB HUNTING

The nursing shortage brings recruiters to you, as many major hospitals send representatives to nursing schools and local job fairs to recruit students. Some even come bearing gifts. This will give you an opportunity to hear what they have to offer and to ask questions in a comfortable environment.

Use the Internet to learn about job openings and places of employment. This helps you compare positions and develop questions to ask nurse recruiters. Find out what you can about the facility, its employees, and the posted job. However, don't rely on these as your only resource. The cost of advertising for a mass audience may be prohibitive for many hospitals, thus the job of your dreams may not be found in cyberspace. Add these methods to your search:

► Check the bulletin boards at school. If something interests you, discuss it with your advisor. Your advisor will help you find more information about the job and facility.

► Ask around. Ask your instructors, friends, and family members about hospitals and other agencies in your area.

► If your school brings in nursing recruiters, make sure to go and listen to them. You'll learn about the facility and have the opportunity to ask questions.

► Go to career fairs. You'll be able to talk to numerous recruiters, allowing you to compare and contrast their facilities. Career fairs also give you the opportunity to network with other nurses; ask them career questions, too!

► Join the Student Nurses Association and go to conferences. This gives you more networking opportunities and access to career opportunities.

Sample Job Announcement

FACILITY: STATE PSYCHIATRIC HOSPITAL

TITLE: PSYCHIATRIC REGISTERED NURSE

PROGRAM: ADULT PSYCHIATRIC DEPARTMENT

POSITION RESPONSIBILITIES: Seeking highly motivated nurse for a 20-bed adult chronic psychiatric illness unit. Responsibilities include:

- Psychiatric and physical assessments
- Administration of medications
- Work as part of an interdisciplinary team in developing treatment and aftercare plans for clients
- Conduct psychoeducation groups

QUALIFICATIONS

- State RN licensure or permit
- Psychiatric experience preferred
- CPR certification

SCHEDULE

- Full-time evenings with one weekend per month
- 8 and 12 hour shifts available

THE NURSING RESUME

With the nursing shortage, chances are good that you will get a job. But your goal is to get the job you want. Your resume acts as your calling card, so you want nurse recruiters to know that you are well qualified, even if you have not graduated from nursing school yet. Be sure to include your clinical rotations, certifications, any work experience (nursing-related or not), and any activity that highlights your experience and/or shows you are a hard worker.

Sample Nursing Student Resume

Your name

Your address

Your city, state, and zip code

Your phone number

Your cell phone number

Your e-mail address

GOAL:

Obtain position as a registered nurse in an emergency department.

EDUCATION:

Baccalaureate degree in nursing with a minor in health administration from Center University, New York, New York

Expected date of graduation: May 2010

GPA: 3.75

Clinical experiences:

Emergency Nursing: Center University Medical Center, New York, New York

Critical Care: Center University Medical Center, New York, New York

Leadership: Center University Medical Center, New York, New York

Adult Health: Center University Medical Center, New York, New York

Women's Health: Community Hospital, White Plains, New York

Pediatric Nursing: Community Hospital, White Plains, New York

Psychiatric Nursing: Mountain Lodge Center, Scarsdale, New York

Community Health Nursing: County Health Department, Westchester, New York

High School Diploma from Center High School, Yonkers, New York

Graduated May 2006 with honors

GPA: 3.88

CERTIFICATIONS:

CPR: American Red Cross 2009

IV Therapy: 2009

Certified Nurses Aide (CNA): 2008

WORK EXPERIENCE:

2008–2009: Nurse's Aide: Community Hospital, New York, New York

2006–2008: Unit Clerk: Community Hospital, New York, New York

2004–2006: Cashier: Dollar Days Minimart

RELEVANT EXPERIENCES:

2008–2009: Assisted with data collection on Dr. Smith's Emergency Room Nurses
Study

2006–2009: Student Nurses Association; President, 2008–2009

2006–2009: Volunteer at The Corner Soup Kitchen

2006–2009: Volunteer for Habitat for Humanity

THE JOB INTERVIEW

First impressions count. Treat each interview as if it were the last job on earth. Plan ahead: Learn about the institution; make a list of questions to ask the recruiter and one of possible questions a recruiter may ask you. Practice interviewing. If no one is home to help, use a mirror.

Questions Nurse Recruiters May Ask

- Tell me a little about yourself.
- Why are you interested in this position?
- Why do you feel you are qualified for this position?
- What do you feel you can offer to this position?
- What do you see as your main strengths?
- What do you see as areas you need to improve?
- How do you manage difficult clinical situations?
- Where do you see yourself five years from now?

When the interview day arrives, relax. Use your stress management skills: Take deep breaths and do relaxation exercises, get plenty of sleep the previous night, and eat a good breakfast. Dress in your interview suit and wear sensible shoes and accessories. Arrive early for the interview, allowing plenty of time for traffic congestion and parking problems. Be courteous;

shake hands and thank the recruiter for taking time to interview you. Project confidence; sit up straight and don't fidget. Don't chew gum or bite your nails.

After the interview, send a thank-you note, again thanking the recruiter for their time. It's polite, and it refreshes your name in their mind. Make a follow-up call to inquire about the state of your application.

PROMOTING YOURSELF AND YOUR CAREER

Nurses rarely think of promoting themselves, but recognition is critical for professional survival, especially if you plan on furthering your career. Self-promotion also allows you to reach more clients, especially if you enjoy client teaching.

Here are some helpful hints to get you started:

Build on your niche. Use your niche to give you something specific to promote.

Realize that self-promotion takes time, and budget it. Figure out how much time you want to devote to marketing yourself and mark it on your calendar.

Learn marketing skills. Marketing means more than providing hands-on care. You will need to develop your speaking and writing skills. Brush up on what you learned in Communication and Composition 101. Read consumer magazines to learn colloquial style, and listen to what your clients want to learn about when you teach and counsel them. You may want to consider taking an adult learning or continuing education course. Online companies, like www.ed2go, offer inexpensive, quick courses on communication, writing, and marketing skills.

Be accessible. Have a working answering machine or voice mail with a professional greeting, and an e-mail account. Fun e-mail addresses and greetings may be nice for friends and family, but not for business. If you still do not have a computer, set up an account where you work or at the local library. Invest in a cell phone with voice mail so you can make and receive calls practically anywhere. You can devote a pay-as-you-go cell phone to business purposes.

Focus. Market what you do best and are most passionate about, such as diabetic teaching, stress management, or parenting skills. Essentially, create a brand name for yourself. Generic packaging is not very appealing or memorable. Jane Doe, RN, will be better recognized as Jane Doe, RN, the wound, ostomy, and continence nurse. People do not care about what you do for a living; they care about what you do for them, and you can show off your credentials.

Get business cards that list your name, title, phone number, and e-mail address. Carry them with you at all times, and hand them out every chance you get. Keep the cards simple and professional. You can make them on your computer, purchase them at an office supply store, or buy them online at Web sites such as www.vistaprint.com.

Network. Join your state nurses association. Attend local as well as national conferences and nursing meetings. Get to know people, including the exhibitors, and let them know that you are available for speaking engagements, writing assignments, consultations, or referrals.

Volunteer your time. Volunteer at blood pressure screening clinics for the homeless. Speak at a PTA meeting, library event, or community meeting. Word-of-mouth advertising is a powerful marketing tool.

Write. Send letters to the editor, write a column for your local paper, and submit clinical articles to professional journals. If you have good writing skills, consider writing for consumer magazines or even writing a book about your topic.

Create a website, blog, or MySpace page. Many Internet service providers have free, but limited, space that you can use. Better yet, contact a Web designer and get help creating a site that provides information for consumers and healthcare providers. Let readers know that you are available to speak on your topic.

Develop a newsletter. You can make a simple one with your word processing software and e-mail it to friends, family, and coworkers and ask them to promote it. Make it interactive, so that readers can contact you and be heard. People love to express their viewpoints, and providing them with a forum to do so will certainly help you get your name noticed.

Contact local radio and television stations. Pitch yourself and your focus topics to them. Send a brief biography and a photo (preferably a professionally photographed headshot), as well as a bulleted write-up about what you have to offer their audience. Learn to be comfortable in front of a camera and microphone, and learn to be as interesting as you are informative.

Look for tie-ins. If a new baby product store is opening, contact management to see if you can assist by talking to new mothers about infant care. Represent yourself to the media as an expert available for interviews when events occur that relate to your focus area.

Send out press releases. These should inform people of your achievements as well as your upcoming speaking events. Start with having passed NCLEX and gotten your license. An effective press release is one or two pages of double-spaced text with an attention-grabbing headline and lead paragraph. The lead paragraph should contain the "who, what, when, where, and how" of your achievement or event. Customize the release for the audience, and keep it interesting. Be sure to include your photo and contact information.

Be patient, but persistent.

Stay passionate. Marketing is not for everyone, but most nurses have the basic skills to get better recognition for themselves—and the profession. So get out and get noticed.

CHAPTER seven

A JOB is just a job without meaning. Marybeth Gabriel wraps things up nicely: "I switched to nursing after graduating with a Bachelor's in Health Science. Most of the jobs that I looked into required a nursing degree. I thought, "Why not? I'll just keep going to school." I had done my internship for my bachelor's in cardiac rehab with nurses and had loved that, so I assumed that I would love nursing as well. The thing about the nursing is that it's *hard*. It's time-consuming, you lose sleep, you study more than you've ever studied for anything in your life, you take care of some of the sickest people you've ever seen, and you learn a lot of life lessons. It's the most rewarding thing that you could do, and I love it."

Both students and seasoned nurses share what it means for them to be a nurse (and some helpful survival tips). They all took the gloves off; you will read about the bad with the good, the tears and the triumphs, the pain and the joys. Most of all you'll read that despite the late-night studying, the mountains of paperwork, and the hectic schedules, knowing that you make a difference in people's lives every day is what nursing really means.

My Journey as a Nursing Student, by Amy Carbone

When I was just 17, a senior in high school, I discovered that I was pregnant. I was excited but scared, I knew that I wanted to provide a hopeful and promising life for my unborn child. Throughout my pregnancy I got to interact with several nurses who were compassionate, caring, and committed to my health and care. This is when I discovered I wanted to be a nurse. After graduating from high school I enrolled in college to begin my career. I found it challenging to balance being a full-time mother, fiancée, daughter, and student. I learned how to manage time and ask for help, even when I didn't want to. Thankfully, I had a strong support group of people who wanted to see me succeed. I never thought I would enjoy school, until I started the nursing program. The friendships I have made are everlasting, and the people I have met along the way are nothing short of inspiring. Aside from my professors, who have all been amazing role models, the patients, the direct care, the trust each individual client grants you is a feeling that words can't describe. I would have never imagined that complete strangers can bring tears to your eyes as you watch them go through an illness, form bonds with these patients, and understand that they are not just patients—they are people. People who feel pain, who suffer, who cry, who get embarrassed; these people have kept me wanting to be a nurse. These individuals have kept me committed to my ultimate goal, in the hope that I will meet more like them in the future. I find the workload demanding and difficult at times, and sometimes I feel guilty that I'm not there all the time with my daughter. It's taken me a while, but I've learned how to do it all, be a mother, a fiancée, a student, and a friend—and eventually, an excellent nurse.

An Honorable Profession, by Caitlin Van Brunt

Being a nurse is honorable and rewarding, to say the least. Nurses must be vigilant at all times; their days will never be boring and are filled with unexpected surprises. They must be tremendously knowledgeable about every aspect of their patient, and be prepared for any situation. Nurses have grave responsibilities throughout their day and must balance their hectic personal lives as wives, husbands, mothers, and fathers with a tedious and overwhelming daily workload. This profession truly is a full-time job of caring for others. Nurses carry their caring personalities into all parts of their lives. Nursing is one career that is worked for from the beginning of student nursing until the day a well-seasoned nurse retires. Coming home from a day of work is extremely fulfilling.

Almost everyone knows a nurse. When a nurse is asked about his or her day, even the best attempt to describe it will not serve any justice to what the nurse really does all day. Even the smallest efforts of a nurse yield big outcomes. She or he may have made the day easier for a new nurse, helped a post-op patient take the first steps with a newly replaced knee, taught a patient how to give herself medications, prevented a medication error of the doctor or pharmacy to ensure a patient's safety, helped deliver a baby and instill confidence into new parents, sat at the bedside of a newly diagnosed cancer patient attending chemotherapy for the first time, advocated on behalf of the patient with other members of a disciplinary team, and thought critically about the patient every step of the way. The nurse is undoubtedly the backbone of the hospital. He is the "go to" person, the one everyone knows will care about the patient as a whole. So, describing to someone that a nurse has passed medications, or helped someone to the bathroom during the day, does not suffice as a true explanation of what was really done in one day of nursing. The nurse is constantly anticipating challenges and problems and intervening to ensure the safety of the patient and quality care, while having the utmost concern for the patient and his family. It is not every day people can come home from work and feel they have truly accomplished something, but it certainly is every day that nurses can come home and say they have changed someone's life. This is truly an honorable profession.

The Right Choice, by Christina Haggerty

My decision to become a nurse will forever be a choice made for *me*. Not a day goes by when I don't think, "What the heck did I get myself into? Do I really want to be a nurse?" In my times of worrying how much I might not have what it takes, I remind myself of days past. Days where patients' simple words of encouragement and gratitude touched my life are more than the fading memories of time I spent at their bedside.

The Best Two Years of My Life, by Alexandra Karlgut

There comes a point in everyone's life when it is time to choose a career. At 20 years of age I was accepted into a nursing program. Never in my life have I been so challenged in all aspects—mental, social, emotional, spiritual, and even physical. The extremely long study hours coupled with traveling to clinical and night classes have only made me a stronger person. At the end of the day I wanted to give up because it seemed impossible to get everything done and still manage to get a little sleep and time with family. Honestly, it has been the hardest two years of my life. I am pretty sure I cried at least every other day; however, these years have been the most rewarding. I would remember how thankful a new mother was for teaching her about signs and symptoms of infection to watch for in her newborn baby; how an elderly man laughed at my cheesy jokes and told me that I made his day; and how a simple smile can touch a person's heart deeper than anyone can imagine.

Not only has my nursing program university provided me with great clinical and class experience but it has also given me the opportunity of a lifetime. This opportunity was to travel to another country. I went to the Dominican Republic with faculty and five other students. When I came back I realized that every country has its own unique needs; however, there should be universal standards of healthcare. These standards should guide healthcare professionals in providing the best possible care for the patients within their own unique setting and culture. Sending students and faculty to these developing countries helped them to come one baby step closer to improving their own system and embracing universal standards of care with each passing day. I also recognized that missionaries and medical teams should not alter the system but can empower natives to learn, to pass on that learning to others, and progress to a higher level of knowledge, understanding, and healthcare delivery.

I need to mention that nursing became my life and a part of who I am today. Not a day goes by that I don't think about those poor children in the Dominican, or the time I spent in the hospital, all the different things I have seen, and all the wonderful people I have met as a student nurse. I have learned so much and I have my professors and clinical instructors to thank. I also have my family, my future husband, and my friends to thank. Without this support system it would have been more difficult to get to where I am today.

Going Greek and Gearing Up for Nursing, by Andrea Randrup

As a 19-year-old nursing sophomore, I have to admit that growing up I always had a "Doctors are greater than nurses" mentality. However, after getting older, hearing the feedback from other health professionals, and experiencing the environment first-hand through volunteer work, I gained a new respect for nurses. I came to realize that they are the backbone of the hospital because they care for the patient holistically.

Being a Filipino American, I grew up with a lot of parental and cultural influences. My parents both worked at hospitals and so urged me to go into the medical field as well. In the Philippines, where poverty is high and education isn't universally accessible, receiving a college education is a privilege. The goal is to choose a path that will benefit not just yourself but others around you. Hence, why nursing is such a popular course. To many Filipinos, the chance of becoming a nurse opens many doors of opportunity, leading them out of an unfavorable lifestyle and into a job that can provide. With nursing always in demand, being a nurse allows many Filipinos to emigrate and work abroad.

Going into college, I knew I wanted to go into a health profession—and not completely due to my family's input. I believe I have a calling to help those in need and I can truly see myself being a caretaker. I didn't know whether to go the biology route or the nursing route. In the end, I applied to be a nursing student. I figured I can always continue on to medical school with nursing as my undergraduate major or at least pursue a higher degree in nursing—hopefully, becoming a nurse practitioner or even going into a new program I heard about in which I could receive a doctorate of nursing. I'll have to see after the next two years, though, considering I have yet to take genuine nursing courses.

College life has been pretty manageable so far. I'm a member of a couple of organizations on campus and still manage to keep up with my work and find time for myself. I joined Kappa Phi Lambda, an Asian-interest sorority, in my freshman year and have found that being in the Greek life comes with many preconceptions. Because of the media, Greeks are typically portrayed as the socialites of the campus who do nothing but party it up and drink it down. I've accepted that as an assumption some people will make about me but I'd like to set the record straight. Being in a sorority or fraternity is all up to the individual who joins it. Greek life is what you make of it and there are many more pros to outbalance the cons movies and television programs have placed on them. Being in a sorority has helped me manage my time better;

it's helped me form bonds with other undergraduates in my major as well as alumni who are now nurses in the real world; it's allowed me to understand that responsibility comes with some sacrifice; that the needs of the whole should always be on my mind; and yes, as cheesy as it sounds, it's a group of girls I can relate to on different levels. It's true that Greeks can have fun but we hold ourselves to a very important principle of academic excellence, too. Personally, I understand that I attend a university and my parents work hard to pay my tuition in order for me to receive a good education, and there are many other students who are able to balance extracurricular activities with classwork. I just want others to know that being Greek does not mean you have to throw away your study habits.

Again, of course, I have yet to experience what nursing truly has in store for me and I have a semester left to hone my time management skills and tendency to procrastinate. I said I make time for my work and get things done but sometimes it happens the night before or a couple minutes before they're due. Haha, I am human after all.

What It Is Like to Be a Student Nurse, by Ashley French

Have you ever heard the saying, "Take a break from having a life, become a nursing student"? That pretty much sums up the workload end of being a nursing student. On a more serious note, being a nursing student is challenging, stressful, and demanding, but it is also very rewarding. The journals become tedious and the care plans become repetitive, but it is worth all of the work when your patient says, "Thank you, you helped me feel better today."

In order to get my point across, I am describing one of my clinical days. It was my first day giving medications in my Adult Health I clinical. My professor hadn't known me very well, and I wanted to prove that I knew my medications and that I had picked up efficient nursing skills from my summer externship. I was just introducing myself to my patient as my professor walked into the room. My patient had been very angry over a conversation she had with the primary nurse, and had been taking her frustrations out on me. Unprepared for such a situation, I panicked for a short moment, collected my thoughts, and managed to successfully calm down my patient. After the morning chaos, my patient had opened up to me and apologized for the way she had acted. I spent much of the day with her. She had an extensive list of medications and needed wound care on both of her lower extremities. She also needed point-of-cares, breathing treatments, and to be ambulated. After a busy day of clinical, I returned to my patient's room to let her know that I was leaving. To my surprise, she became up-set and told me that she wanted to talk to me. As I had done throughout the day, I sat down to listen to my patient. She told me that she had admired my patience and ea-gerness to learn. She then gave me the best compliment a nursing student could get, and told me that I was going to be an excellent nurse.

Likes and Dislikes, by Ashley Panaro

Being a student nurse has been an exciting and scary experience. During my years of schooling, I have had some likes and dislikes. The items that I liked were that I met a lot of good friends and encountered many different situations. The amount that I have learned in the last four years has been more intense and exciting than any other schooling I have done. I also enjoyed the freedom the professors give you once they are certain of your abilities. You are able to care for patients and gain experience because you are treated like you are an ac-tual nurse.

The items that I disliked about being a student nurse were as follows. Some of the coursework was grueling and difficult to keep up with. There were times when I felt as though I would never succeed. Also, being a student nurse, despite what I mentioned earlier, you are treated as though you do not know anything. At these times you feel as though your school was for nothing. There are not a lot of things that I dislike about being a student nurse. It is definitely one of the most promising decisions I have ever made, and I have learned a lot from it.

Finding My Niche, by Essie Lee

The experience I had working as a secretary during the summer after my freshman year solidified my decision to become a nurse. Because I was working full-time, I quickly developed a close relationship with my coworkers. One fellow employee (whom I shall refer to as M) in particular changed my perspective on life and health care. M was a single mother with one child and no financial support from her family. Despite the fact that she was unable to speak English, she had spent all her money on travel expenses from Mexico to New York City. Her duties were to keep the place tidy and to empty the wastebaskets on a daily basis. One particular day while she was completing her usual tasks, she cut herself on a razor during an attempt to remove the trash. M was bleeding profusely and her cut was deep enough that the wound would require several stitches to stop the bleeding. But surprisingly, many of our coworkers were reluctant to help, because it turned out that M was an illegal immigrant. None of the employees wanted to assist her with seeking medical attention because they were concerned about colliding with the law due to her immigration status. The mere fact that someone was severely injured and others did not want to help made me realize that perhaps there may be others in the same predicament as M, people in dire need of medical attention but unable to seek it due to their low income or immigration status. These five minutes redefined my definition of a nurse, someone who gives full and utmost care to a patient regardless of his or her race, ethnicity, financial, and immigration status. It does not matter who is injured, only that someone is injured and is in desperate need of medical attention.

When I returned to school that following fall semester to begin my sophomore year, I was motivated more than ever to become a nurse. I began to take all the prerequisites required prior to starting the nursing program. I decided to take both winter and summer classes to complete all the required courses in time. Once I had begun taking my core nursing courses during my junior year, I started searching for a summer externship to experience the many different fields that nursing had to offer. Luckily, I discovered my niche at a hospital that was funded by the government in New York City. Because it was a public hospital, immigration status and medical insurance were not questioned when the patients arrived. But what further enhanced my determination to become a nurse was my placement at a hospice unit within the externship. Prior to the externship, I was unaware that palliative care existed in nursing. At first I had difficulty adjusting to the idea of caring for a patient when death was imminent, rather than aggressively treating a patient to avoid death. But the nurses taught me to see that the patient would be resting in comfort during his or her remaining time. They allowed me to realize that with palliative care, a nurse can take a negative situation and make it the most positive time remaining for both the patients and their family members. Once I completed my summer externship and returned to continue my nursing studies, I asked to observe the hospice unit during my off-unit days while I was completing my clinical rotations. With the helpful guidance I received from all the nurses in every hospice unit I was able to encounter, I became confident that my personality corresponded well with palliative care.

I currently have one semester remaining at the university, but the past events that have taken place throughout my college years have led to self-discovery. Both my experiences at my summer externship and clinical rotations at school have allowed me to realize who I am and what field of nursing would be most suitable. I highly encourage other students to observe the many different fields that nursing has to offer; perhaps it may open doors that were thought to be nonexistent.

On Being a Student Nurse, by Lindsay Giordano

What is it like to be a student nurse? Several words come to mind when I think about my four years in nursing school: determination, hard work, maturity, and responsibility. All of these words exemplify the personality of a student nurse. When I entered school for nursing, I was always told it was going to be challenging, with long study hours and the responsibility of people's lives in your hands. Although the thought was scary I was determined to get through it. The truth about being a student nurse, to put it simply, is that it is difficult. I have never met someone who goes through nursing school and says it was easy and not at all challenging. Being a student nurse has taught me all different kinds of responsibility and has helped me with my personal life more than any experience I have been through. It has shown me I can do anything that I put my mind to and I have become a much more mature person through my experiences at school, at clinical, and working in the hospital as an extern. Through my experience I have realized that it takes a certain person to be a student nurse—someone who has the drive to succeed in life, wants to help people, deeply cares about others, and is patient and understanding. Being a student nurse is not easy, but it is definitely worth it.

Why I Switched to Nursing, by Faye Zhong

A career in nursing was never part of my plan for my future until my junior year in college. Throughout my college career I had tried to live up to my parents' and siblings' expectations by becoming more of what they wanted me to be, and nursing was certainly not on top of their list of prestigious future careers. Prior to entering nursing school, I was studying economics and I realized that I feared and dreaded the concept of sitting in a cubicle and staring into a computer screen from 9 to 5 for the rest of my career life. I realized that I couldn't pursue a career in which the nature of the profession lacks meaning and personal fulfillment.

As cliché as it may sound, I truly do feel that my decision to become a nurse was primarily fueled by the satisfaction I would get from helping others. Being able to make someone else feel better either physically or emotionally really does give me a sense of pleasure and fulfillment as I pursue a career in nursing. My individual characteristics played an important role in choosing this profession. As a nursing student and as a future nurse, I strongly feel that without compassion, the desire to want to help others, and most importantly having tremendous patience, the quality of care and the relationship between nurse and patient would indisputably be affected. My motivations and incentives as a nursing student come from my personal desire for the need to provide optimal quality of care that we as future nurses could advocate for and potentially deliver to our patients. As a student nurse, I believe that my compassion and desire to help others gave me a greater sense of pleasure and fulfillment in the nursing program, which in turn motivates me to become a better student and helps drive me to provide better care to patients.

Despite the benefits of job security and a good income in the nursing profession, my advice for those who are thinking about switching into the nursing field for the sole purpose of these incentives is for them to have some basic understanding and knowledge of the nursing profession prior to making their decision. Despite these advantages, nursing may not be suitable for everyone. Some might find nursing to be fulfilling while others might feel miserable and discontented; however, nursing is a very broad profession with endless opportunities and varieties of specialty fields.

The Military View, by Howie Romans

For most, nursing school is typically a fluid progression through the course of four rewarding, yet challenging, years. In what I jokingly reference as the extended degree program, my experience in nursing school has presented both unique challenges and rewards, courtesy of my proud service to my country, as a member of the U.S. military. The combination of nursing education with military training and experience, I sincerely believe, has contributed to another dimension, of me, that most may be unable to fully understand. These experiences have helped me to fully realize the invaluable role that nurses play in not just tending to physical ailments, but also to caring for the whole person, in a genuine, holistic manner.

Immediately following the terrorist attacks of September 11, I had the honor of serving overseas, in Afghanistan, alongside some of the best soldiers and marines in the U.S. military. My education had to be put on hold. It was during this time of being fearful and experiencing the casualties of war firsthand, that an immediate change in my major to nursing was, without a doubt, in complete alignment with what I knew I wanted to do with my life. While some people spend a lifetime trying to figure out what they want to do with their lives, in hindsight, nursing was the clearest choice I have ever made. My service in New Orleans, Louisiana, immediately following the national disaster known as Hurricane Katrina, only served to validate, and reinforce, that decision.

Instead of looking at my situation filled with bitterness and anger, thanks to my military service nursing school has been even that much more interesting and rewarding. As entire classes have come and gone I've had the opportunity to meet some great students, who, I know, have gone on to be tremendous contributors to society. I have always been convinced that two of the most demanding professions are that of a soldier and that of a nurse. In my case, I chose both, and I wouldn't have it any other way. The art of soldiering has instilled in me great discipline, and leadership, that I have been able to carry on into my nursing career so far.

PhD Bound, by Jahaira Capellan

Nursing for me is the perfect profession because of the wide range of opportunities that it offers. Nursing allows you to work in a variety of disciplines, and it is flexible enough to adapt to your changing needs as an individual as you continue to grow and develop. It is a profession that has an impact on so many lives. As a nurse you focus not only on the client's ailment, but also on the person as a whole. A nurse understands that there is so much more to a person than just lying in a hospital bed and that many factors that aren't written on the chart can affect a person's health. These factors are important because they can help you to determine the best plan of care for a particular client, thereby increasing the likelihood that the client will have better outcomes.

I personally would like to further my education and get a PhD in behavioral health research. This will allow me to maximize my ability to help people. It will give me the opportunity to practice clinically as a family nurse practitioner, teach, and do research on child abuse. I am interested in researching the risk factors and implications that such a traumatic experience has on kids, as well as the different kinds of interventions that can be established to prevent child abuse from occurring.

Tips for Success, by Jessica Beyer

My greatest tip for future nursing students: Know yourself and why you are becoming a nurse. If care over cure is the foundation of nursing education, then build your studying around that principle. The vast amount of information that incorporates the nursing curriculum will never be fully remembered, but prioritizing what is important and what will make a difference for your patients should be burned into memory. You determine your goals and outcomes, so study hard to make it worth *your* while. Nursing is about caring for the needs of others, so forget the overachievers who want to beat out everyone, and study for your own future patients. Studying isn't a competition; it is part of the job description. Ask yourself why you care about this profession, and do what makes you happy. The studying will naturally fall into place if the dedication is there.

My Father's Inspiration, by John Gao

When I entered the nursing program as a freshman, my father had been diagnosed with throat and brain cancer several years before. He was the single reason that ignited my desire for nursing. Others would ask me why I became a nurse, and not a doctor, and my answer was always, "I do not know." Many things held me back from what other people would consider bigger dreams such as being a doctor. At the time I doubted my potential, my own intelligence, and the fear of an unknown future, as any high school senior would. Coming from an immigrant family of five and lacking resources, the choice of nursing was a big enough leap for me. Whether one would conventionally consider being a doctor superior to being a nurse, I did not care. I wanted to help people, especially my father.

It was not until the beginning of my sophomore year that experience shook me deeply. Two weeks before the semester began, my father was admitted to the hospital. Seeing my father in a hospital bed is still indescribable. Taking rounds by switching off with my brother and sister to keep my father company affirmed my decision to become a nurse. There was no doubt that nursing was for me. As my father got better the nurses expressed their joy, whereas the resident doctor, who had already given up hope, was surprised he even got better. The summer ended and I was reluctant to go back to school, but I did what I thought my father would want from me, to do my best at school. A few weeks later a phone call came in telling me my father had passed away.

There is now a struggle every day. I know I'm not the only one who struggles with loss, and others may struggle with things greater than loss. As a nurse, I can empathize and encourage others to stay strong. I was taught in nursing that until you are healed, you cannot heal others. But I find that to be incorrect in my life. In my view, if one is strong enough, then one can help others find strength within themselves. My strength comes from my struggle with loss. I know that my father loves me and knows that I'm capable of doing great things. It is up to me to do what I was made to do.

As a junior male in the nursing program, if I were asked once again why become a nurse and not a doctor, I would say, "Who cares why this or that, the better question to ask is, what personal experience did you encounter that led to the decision to become a nurse?"

Moving Up, by Katherine Levis

I've always known I wanted to work in the medical field in some way. Being a single mother of two children and living on $12 an hour while working in the hospital is not what I planned for the rest of my life. I obtained my associate degree, but knew that if I wanted stability and a real medical profession, nursing was the way to go. I started off in the nursing program at a community college, which I really enjoyed. However, I knew that getting my bachelor's degree in nursing was a better fit.

I transferred to a university and began the nursing program there. I have to say this was the best decision I could have ever made. I am not saying that it has been easy because it hasn't. It is a difficult program even for the traditional college student. It's very time-consuming, with clinical, labs, and paperwork. There were many days when I didn't know if I was going to get through the program, but I kept going. It has been a wonderful experience, though. You could not ask for a better mix of professors and instructors, who are all professionals in the field—caring is imprinted in their DNA. They understand that life happens and things come up, as they were in our shoes once. I enjoy the fact that we get to know our peers, sharing many of the same classes. We all can relate to what the others are going through, making our connections with each other stronger.

I currently have one semester left and will graduate with my bachelor's. I feel that I will be ready and prepared to take the nursing licensure exam. I ultimately want to continue my education and eventually get my master's degree. Since there are so many fields in nursing, I want to be able to focus on what area I enjoy. I hope experience will provide me with the direction I want to take and help me decide how to focus my master's. Nursing is an honorable and rewarding profession, and I feel so lucky to be a small part of it.

Graduation Is Just the Beginning, by Krista Wachendorfer

It seems like just yesterday I discovered that I was accepted into nursing school. Rumors about the hard work needed in the particular major were acknowledged but not truly understood until endless amounts of work began to pile up week after week. Reading long detailed textbook chapters, practicing NCLEX questions, solving dosage calculation problems, creating care maps for patients, and writing assigned journals for scheduled clinical days became a lifestyle. After many stressful days and nights of trying to complete the demands of nursing school, questions arose that focused on the thought, "Is this really worth it?" I am now a senior-year nursing student with one semester left of nursing school, and I can answer that question with an honest "*yes!*"

I can reflect on the moments spent with the patients and the endless paperwork becomes forgettable. Nursing is a career that allows you to drastically intervene into someone's life. As a nursing student I was introduced to this and my job was to lead them toward a more positive direction. I have taken care of a variety of patients who range from a healthy mother who had just given birth to her first-born to an old man only hours away from his final breaths. At my final stage of school, I don't feel the anxiety that was felt before a big test or challenging question asked in a previous class. I now understand that the work was hard because of the rewards it is leading me to. I have had and will continue to have the opportunity to be beside someone during the most vulnerable moments—moments that only a nurse can understand. To be able to say that I will be taking care of someone's life is so moving to me in many ways. However, what is even more amazing to me is that as a student I can say that this is just the beginning!

Touching Lives, by Laura Garrison

The experience of being a nursing student is extraordinary, and unlike any other type of college student there is. This time in my life has been one filled with self-discovery and realizations about the world. Commitment and responsibility are two virtues that nursing students have to become very familiar with, and the level at which my nursing classmates and I embody these is astonishing to me. We have come to be wise beyond our years, for we have seen people suffering. Most students our age do not have this opportunity. We have felt what it is like to have someone trust us with their health, and allow us into their personal world and space. It truly is a gift. The respect that the patients have for us and the nursing profession is tangible. Although college is not always smooth sailing, and the emotional roller coaster metaphor seems so fitting here, I know I am expressing the feelings of most of my classmates when I say that nursing school has facilitated my coming into my life's calling. It has channeled the caring personalities we have into skilled work with people who need our help the most. As a second semester senior with graduation not five months away, I can see the light at the end of the tunnel. Nursing school has been an amazing experience, and its teachings will shape the type of nurse I will be for the rest of my life. While all of my fellow college students are searching for jobs in today's market, I am looking for the right job; a job that will allow me to use all of my nursing skills, both clinical and interpersonal, to the fullest. I only hope that I can touch as many lives as the nursing faculty I have been privileged to work with.

A Close Shave, by Laura Benjamin

Being a nursing student is a stressful, emotional ride. It isn't the same as English class where you hand in your paper and go home. You interact with real people undergoing real medical problems who are facing their own mortality, usually for the first time. Just as important as honing your clinical skills is learning what to do with the things you see every day, or one day you won't be able to face going into work even one more time. While the downs are pretty low, nothing beats the little thing you do for that one person that garners so much appreciation that you go home completely high. Once, I shaved a man's face. He was too sick to do it himself. He was so grateful, he couldn't stop talking about it all shift long and tried to make his son pay me for it. It took 10 minutes and it made someone on death's door feel like a million bucks—you can't get that in other professions.

Massaging a Second Career, by Lisa Daly

I had been a massage therapist for eight years when I decided to pursue a BSN degree. I had enjoyed working with people and helping to develop goals for them to eliminate any pain they may have been suffering. Since I was self-employed and running my own office, money was always running out the door faster than in. Gaining my RN would give me more opportunities for employment. With my massage therapy background, I understand the power of the simple touch on the hand, or the light pat on the back. I have enjoyed my education a great deal so far in the nursing program and I have applied much of the knowledge to my massage practice.

Adding "full-time student" to my already full schedule as a wife, mother, and business owner has been challenging. It has added a great strain at home, I will not lie. Getting up earlier in the morning as opposed to staying up late does help out. Getting the boys ready for school the night before instead of in the morning adds to the organization. However, up here in the Northeast, snow days for the kids pop up out of nowhere, so depending on them being at school every day is not advised.

One piece of advice I have for anyone starting nursing school is to make friends with your peers. These people are going though the same rigorous program you are. Having someone to talk to makes the rough days easier to deal with. Also, although you may have made some great friends, never forget that you are solely responsible for your performances on tests and projects. It is up to you to keep up with course materials and lectures and maximize your educational outcome.

From Tears to Triumph, by Mandy Lorenz

Being a nursing student brings about many feelings of exhilaration, as well of feelings of being small and afraid. Nursing school is scary. There is so much to learn and so little time. You will be responsible for someone's life someday. How will you ever do it? How can you ever succeed when you need to know 10 chapters of material in one week? How can you ever recall the steps to resuscitate someone in cardiac arrest? Are you really that dumb? Is your mind made of Teflon? No! The hectic, scary, fast-paced, overwhelming schedule and curriculum of nursing students make them great nurses, leaders, advocates, and above all, flexible. You need to feel small and scared to become great. You need to be pushed and almost provoked into tears to get a grip on your dreams of becoming a fabulous nurse. Overcoming all of these awful feelings brings you to a place where exhilaration takes over. You are excited to get to clinical at 6 A.M. the next day. You become determined to take the next exam. At this point, you've mastered the impossible schedules and you begin to pull the bits and pieces together and the big picture is now clear!

Being a nursing student is one of the most fulfilling achievements of my life. I graduate in May with my class. These four years of my life have brought me full circle. I started as a shy, quiet, and extremely timid freshman and have bloomed into a confident, loud, bright, and enthusiastic senior. Nursing is now my life and my life is so much better than I could have imagined!

The Reality of Being a Nursing Student, by Mary Kate McFarland

Upon being accepted into the nursing program at my university I had no idea what lay ahead of me. Becoming a nurse has been the most emotionally, mentally, and physically difficult task I have ever undertaken. When first starting out in the program I became overwhelmed by the course load. However, as I have progressed in the curriculum, I am finding the classroom aspect of nursing school to be the easy part. Caring for patients has presented more challenges to me than I could have ever imagined. Some obstacles are surmountable, others are not. No matter what the outcome, each and every experience I have had as a nursing student has helped to shape me into a more compassionate, competent, and professional health care provider. In just a few short months I am going to have to leave my safety net of instructors and peers and be responsible for functioning independently. Admittedly this thought frightens me, but I am confident that the lessons and skills I have gained during my journey to becoming a nurse will carry me through and help me to thrive as a "green" nurse.

Never Too Late to Be a Nurse, by Michele Summers

I started nursing school in the late 1970s, but never finished. The desire to complete my bachelor's in nursing never left me, even after 27 years of marriage and 20 years of homeschooling my five children. After repeated requests from my youngest daughter, we decided to enroll her and her not-so-eager younger brother in the local middle school. Now was my chance to see what hoops I would need to jump through in order to graduate.

Our family had numerous discussions regarding our role and responsibility changes. Issues we sorted out were menus, shopping, transportation, homework, sports, laundry, and dishes. Creating a chore chart helped us visualize and prioritize what was needed to keep the family running. Everyone from youngest to oldest had an opportunity to choose what they would be willing to do, going around until everything was accounted for. This gave us a basic structure of order with the freedom to trade jobs and flex for each other depending on outside activities and deadlines. Personally, I created a schedule of my classes, clinical, study time, reading assignments, research assistant time, family events, and church volunteer time. Organizing my time this way helped me to reach my goals, readjusting when necessary.

The upside: We were all extremely happy in our new environments. Even my husband had recently started a lifelong dream job as a pastor after 30 years of truck driving. The downside: It was a tiring schedule. Up in the morning, make lunch, everyone do a chore, be at school/work all day, come home and help with homework (my youngest has a reading disability), do dinner and clean up, maybe attend a sport or church event, and study time for me. That first year was a big adjustment. I have three older children who are on their own, and they would help with transportation and go to the kids' games when we needed them.

What helped us was keeping in mind that my schooling was a two-year commitment, that we could do this for four semesters. Something else invaluable is my family's teamwork. Over the years, we emphasized that we are a team, that everyone benefits from our home and family, and that we need to work together. I tell my family and friends at church that the B.S. degree will belong to them as much as me. Experiencing this chapter in my life is encouraging because I realize that other dreams and goals are possible, too.

What It Is Like to Be a Nurse, by Mike Evans

Since I became a registered nurse in 2002, nursing has offered me not only a rewarding career but a way to give back to society. It has allowed me to enter people's lives and touch them, even if only for a brief moment. I have been fortunate enough to be able to both laugh and cry with my patients, often all in the same shift. I have seen births and witnessed deaths, both of which can be very rewarding. Holding someone's hand as they let go from the world can be very emotionally draining for a nurse but also gratifying at the same time, knowing that you have done all you can to help that patient and accompanied him as he entered another place. Nursing has allowed me the opportunity to care for the sick, promote health in the well, and advocate for all.

Nursing has brought me a great many friendships and mentors that I cherish. It has taught me to be selfless and to give more of myself and expect less from others. Nursing has taught me about being a professional and earning respect, not expecting it. Nursing has taught me about leadership and teamwork, both of which are necessary to succeed in this profession. Nursing has taught me that patients need our care at all hours of the day, even if they do not want it or know they need it. Nursing has taught me that as one door closes another door opens, allowing for countless opportunities as a registered nurse. By obtaining advanced education, nursing has allowed me not only to better care for individuals but also to teach others to do the same. Finally, nursing has taught me that there is nothing else in the world that I would rather do.

Making a Difference, by Milt Evans

All too often, we are told that we can and do make a difference in someone's life. However, most of the time, the conscious awareness does not come to fruition. While providing orientation to a class of LPN students, I was approached by one of the students. She shared with me a picture of her beautiful 17-year-old daughter. It was Brianna Leigh! I had been a young student in my obstetrics rotation at school and was assigned a frightened teen single mom. We experienced labor and birth together and I provided her post-delivery care. What a humbling and gratifying serendipitous meeting some 17 years later. It is worth waiting as long as necessary to realize the profession of nursing makes a difference.

Early Risings, by Monica Mazurowski

Becoming a nursing student certainly has its ups and downs. You have moments during clinical where things start clicking and you really help someone and you think, "Wow, this is what I want to do for the rest of my life." Then you have moments in the classroom when you wonder how in the world you will ever make it through the semester, let alone become a nurse. Now that I'm in my senior year, I'm definitely starting to see the light at the end of the tunnel and things are really coming together both in the classroom and in clinical.

One of the biggest challenges I faced throughout nursing school was getting into the swing of clinical. It's not easy to wake up at five o'clock in the morning, be at the hospital at six, and be ready to rattle off all 18 of your patient's medications, why they're here, and five nursing diagnoses for your client. Before nursing school, I didn't start functioning until at least ten o'clock! But somehow you get used to it. I also found it challenging to talk to patients at first. I was so nervous about doing an assessment and concentrating on how many breaths the patient was taking in this minute that I was dumbfounded about what to say. After a few clinicals and listening to other nurses, you definitely get the drift, but there is a sense of awkwardness at first that isn't really recognized by professors. This may sound silly, but my biggest challenge of all was time management. Having to wake up so early for clinical means you need to go to bed early the night before. It's hard to get all of your work done by a reasonable time as it is, not to mention people in the dorms wanting you to socialize and being awake until all hours of the night. And to be completely honest, there were a lot of nights throughout nursing school when I thought, "Gosh, it'd be nice to be an education major for a week."

Army Bound, by Neil Smartschan

I am a male in nursing school. Yes, I have heard it numerous times already from everyone. "Why aren't you going to be a doctor," and I have heard many references to Ben Stiller's infamous character, male nurse Gaylord Focker from the *Meet the Parents* movie. Yet, I am proud to be a nursing student. I feel it takes a special dedication and person to become a successful and motivated nursing student and eventually professional nurse.

After graduation from nursing school I plan on joining the United States Army and becoming a part of the Army Nurse Corps. Not only will I be able to serve my country, but I will also be able to be a nurse at the same time. I have fellow classmates who are planning on joining the Army Nurse Corps as well.

That's me. I am a male nursing student. No, as of now I am not going to be a doctor and, yes, you can call me Gaylord Focker all you want. In what other profession can you go just about anywhere in the country to get a job these days? And in what other major can you go to a student nurse convention and be one of maybe 50 male nursing students? I am proud that I got up at 4:30 A.M. for clinical and provided optimal care to even the most difficult patients. I hope that I have put in the time necessary to become a successful, safe, and prudent registered nurse.

Only the Beginning, by Nicole Russo

Upon entering nursing school, I was eager to learn anything and everything I could that would facilitate my thriving in my future career as a nurse. I would be lying if I said it has been easy. With difficult schedules and long hours of studying combined with the time-consuming preps for clinical and clinical days, it has definitely been a rough ride. There have been numerous times in the past three and a half years in which I have seriously doubted myself in nursing school. It used to give me tremendous amounts of anxiety to believe that as a nurse, in just a few short years, I would be responsible for someone else's life. That said, it has been the most rewarding time of my life thus far and I would not trade it for anything else because of all of the things I have gained from it. Yes, it is a big responsibility, but I soon came to realize that I am not the only nursing student to feel this way and no one in the world can know everything you need to know about nursing while you are still in school. Although nursing school currently provides the knowledge and skills I need in order to start my career, I believe that experience, aside from basic skills and compassion, is the best teacher. In the years to come, I will gain more knowledge and experience, which will help me care for others in the best possible way I am able to.

As a sophomore, when our clinical rotations first began, I can remember how frightened I was as I entered the room of my first patient on a skilled nursing unit. My biggest concern at that time was that I would do something accidentally that would harm my patient instead of helping. Of course, this was a legitimate concern; however, when looking back, I must admit that, unfortunately, sometimes I may have focused more on the nursing skills than on my actual patient. Yes, the skills of nursing are extremely important; medication must be administered safely in the correct dose and in a sterile procedure, sterility must be maintained, but if I have learned one thing it has been that no patient will remember those things. The thing patients will remember is the compassion you had and how they were treated.

Commitment, by Nicole Trama

Being a student nurse is both challenging and rewarding. As students we go through many courses that require both clinical and classroom work. Unlike other majors we spend a great deal of our studies in the field working on different units and sites instead of just being in the classroom. Nursing school is a very hands-on experience with a lot to learn in a short amount of time. The rewarding part of being a student nurse is that we are able to spend a great deal of time working on units and with nurses. We experience first-hand during school what a nurse must complete and how to care for the patients in several different fields of nursing. We are able to care for our own patients under the supervision of registered nurses and our professors and experience the rewards of being a nurse. Although being a student nurse requires a lot of commitment it is something that I enjoy.

The Letter, by Olivia Kurtoglu

During my second med-surge clinical junior year, I took care of an 85-year-old woman who was admitted for treatment of an infected wound. I changed her dressings, assisted her with morning care, amd administered medication. She chatted up a storm. She told me about things that were important to her—her grandchildren, her assisted living friends, and most importantly, her dog. I listened and shared a few stories as well. When it was time to leave for the day, she asked for my address, telling me she would write to me. I wrote my school address on a small sheet of paper and put it in her pants pocket, expecting to never hear from her again.

In nursing school we are told that we may not remember every patient, but it is more than likely your patient will remember you, their nurse (and maybe even their student nurse). About a month later I received a letter in the mail:

Dear Olivia,

I am back at my assisted living apartment. I miss you and hope we can see each other again someday. I am feeling better but cannot leave my apartment. Please write back to me, I can't wait to hear from you. You were my best nurse. Continue to spread your good care and love.

I will certainly never forget this patient. She will certainly never forget me, her *student* nurse. Even as a student, you can make a difference in a patient's life. They *do* appreciate you. This was the best feeling one could ask for in this career.

The Moment, by Rajae Elkirami

Not only was my entrance to the nursing program a challenge, but so was my being in the program. Being a mother of a two-year-old boy and a wife was a challenge, especially since I grew up in a culture where eating outside the home is unacceptable and rare. It is a culture in which you have to cook every day for the family, but thanks to my family's support I made it through. I remember every good and bad moment I passed through during the last two years, but the one I remember best is when I was caring for a lady who was admitted to the hospital because of hyperemesis. I spent most of the shift with her, helping her find some type of food that she might keep in her stomach. When she was discharged at noon, she hugged me as if she knew me for a long time and said, "Thank you, thank you so much for your care and being friendly with me." This is the moment I felt touched and that all the difficulty I went through was worth it. I am ready to be a responsible and caring nurse.

A Freshman's Point of View, by Rosemary Welte

When I started my nursing career as a freshman, I wasn't sure what to expect. It was a big transition from high school to college work, and I wasn't sure whether I could handle it. One of the things I did to help ease into the swing of things, which I would advise anyone else to do who has the same uncertainty about handling coursework at the college level, was to take fewer credits—it really helped me out in the first semester. I got an idea of what the classes were like without feeling like I was flying in too many directions at once, and the extra time for classes helped me to get better grades than I probably would have otherwise. In general, I've tried to keep my credit numbers down ever since, by taking a couple of summer courses to lighten the load during the regular semester, which allows me to focus better and do better in the classes I take.

One of the things I've really enjoyed so far in the nursing program is the size of the school of nursing. Even though I'm only in my second year, I've been able to do a lot of networking with many of the other nursing students, since most of the classes I've been taking are general requirements for all of us. I expect this to help a lot the next couple of years, once my fellow students and I start getting into the hard-core nursing curriculum. It has helped me already to make friends and study partners who I will also be working with in the future. It has even helped when I want to speak with faculty and professors in the nursing program; the school is small enough that people will know me by face, if not by name.

As for the classes themselves, there are ups and downs—classes or professors that I had a hard time with, schedules that weren't always easy, and requirements that were sometimes difficult to juggle—but in general I found that all I really needed to do was focus and put in the time and effort. Sometimes I guess I do this a little overmuch, but it's usually worth it in the end. There have been other times when I have had wonderful classes and great professors, so like anything it's a mixed bag. I'm really looking forward to starting into the core nursing courses, though, since it will bring everything I've been working on these first couple of years into the actual practice of nursing.

One Big Happy Dysfunctional Family, by Samantha Guy

There is no other experience like being a nursing student; it has been the best and worst time of my life. I have had the opportunity to see and do things I never thought I would, I've had the chance to connect with people during a difficult time in their lives and hopefully made them a little better, and I've made friends that I will keep for life. In my senior year of school my fellow classmate described our class perfectly as "a big, loving, dysfunctional family." I wouldn't trade my nursing school years for anything; they have taught me life lessons and, most important, how to be myself.

Passion and Determination, by Sara Rieger

Since being a nursing student I have found that the most important traits to have are passion and determination. Nursing is one of the most challenging majors in college as a student and a person. I like being a nursing student because it exposes me to many different situations that I need to experience in order to become a great nurse. The challenging aspect of being a nursing student is learning time management. There is so much work involved and many deadlines. Learning time management in school will be most helpful when becoming a nurse.

Being a Nurse, by Terri M. Parkin

It doesn't take much to lend a helping hand, help a person cross the street, or give a friend some words of encouragement. But it takes a monumental effort from the kindest person to be a supportive and thoughtful caregiver every day. Nursing is a difficult profession. You put aside personal opinions and issues of selfishness to be the best person you can be, to someone else. It's a beautiful thing and rewarding for those who have the courage to undertake it. I love being a nurse. I enjoy knowing that the smallest things I do, even the ones that I don't think make a difference, do in fact make a difference. People remember the care they received. They remember those consoling moments and times when you made them laugh. It might not always be your name but your presence has had an impact. It took many years and constant perseverance to obtain a nursing degree. There were times when all I wanted to do was give up. What drove me was not just family and friends, but knowing that I have the power to make positive changes in many lives. Nursing is a lifelong commitment of lifelong learning; you never stop. Being a nurse has its struggles like any career. There are moments when all you want to do is cry, but I wouldn't change the feelings of passion, sadness, loneliness, loss, pain, enlightenment, fulfillment, and joy that I feel every day for any other career in the world. You won't realize you chose the right profession until you get out there and do it. Be afraid, be excited, be nervous, but be someone special.

Appendix A

State Boards of Nursing

State boards of nursing regulate nursing practice. They also serve as excellent resources for finding accredited nursing programs.

Alabama Board of Nursing

www.abn.state.al.us

770 Washington Avenue

RSA Plaza, Suite 250

Montgomery, AL 36130-3900

Phone: 334-242-4060

Fax: 334-242-4360

Alaska Board of Nursing

www.dced.state.ak.us/occ/pnur.htm

550 West Seventh Avenue, Suite 1500

Anchorage, AK 99501-3567

Phone: 907-269-8161

Fax: 907-269-8196

American Samoa Health Services
Regulatory Board

http://americansamoa.gov/
department/health.htm

LBJ Tropical Medical Center

Pago Pago, AS 96799

Phone: 684-633-1222

Fax: 684-633-1869

Arizona State Board of Nursing

www.azbn.gov

4747 North 7th Street, Suite 200

Phoenix, AZ 85014-3653

Phone: 602-889-5150

Fax: 602-889-5155

Arkansas State Board of Nursing

www.arsbn.org

University Tower Building

1123 S. University, Suite 800

Little Rock, AR 72204-1619

Phone: 501.686.2700

Fax: 501-686-2714

**California Board of Registered
Nursing**

www.rn.ca.gov

1625 North Market Boulevard,

Suite N-217

Sacramento, CA 95834-1924

Phone: 916-322-3350

Fax: 916-574-8637

**Bureau of Vocational Nursing and
Psychiatric Technicians**

www.bvnpt.ca.gov

2535 Capitol Oaks Drive, Suite 205

Sacramento, CA 95833

Phone: 916-263-7800

Fax: 916-263-7859

Colorado Board of Nursing

www.dora.state.co.us/nursing

1560 Broadway, Suite 1370

Denver, CO 80202

Phone: 303-894-2430

Fax: 303-894-2821

**Connecticut Board of Examiners
for Nursing**

www.state.ct.us/dph

Department of Public Health

410 Capitol Avenue, MS# 13PHO

P.O. Box 340308

Hartford, CT 06134-0328

Phone: 860-509-7624

860-509-7603 (for testing candidates

only)

Fax: 860-509-7553

Delaware Board of Nursing

dpr.delaware.gov/boards/nursing

861 Silver Lake Boulevard

Cannon Building, Suite 203

Dover, DE 19904

Phone: 302-744-4500

Fax: 302-739-2711

**District of Columbia Board of
Nursing**

hpla.doh.dc.gov/hpla/cwp/view,A,1195,

Q,488526,hplaNav,|30661|,.asp

Department of Health

Health Professional Licensing

Administration

717 14th Street, NW, Suite 600

Washington, DC 20005

Phone: 877-672-2174

Fax: 202-727-8471

Florida Board of Nursing

www.doh.state.fl.us/mqa/nursing

Mailing Address:

4052 Bald Cypress Way, BIN C02

Tallahassee, FL 32399-3252

Street Address:

4042 Bald Cypress Way, Room 120

Tallahassee, FL 32399

Phone: 850-245-4125

Fax: 850-245-4172

Georgia State Board of Licensed
   Practical Nurses

www.sos.state.ga.us/plb/lpn

237 Coliseum Drive

Macon, GA 31217-3858

Phone: 478-207-2440

Fax: 478-207-1354

Georgia Board of Nursing

www.sos.state.ga.us/plb/rn

237 Coliseum Drive

Macon, GA 31217-3858

Phone: 478-207-2440

Fax: 478-207-1354

Guam Board of Nurse Examiners

www.dphss.guam.gov

#123 Chalan Kareta

Mangilao, Guam 96913-6304

Phone: 671-735-7407

Fax: 671-735-7413

Hawaii Board of Nursing

www.hawaii.gov/dcca/areas/pvl/
   boards/nursing

Mailing Address:

PVLD/DCCA

Attn: Board of Nursing

P.O. Box 3469

Honolulu, HI 96801

Street Address:

King Kalakaua Building

335 Merchant Street, 3rd Floor

Honolulu, HI 96813

Phone: 808-586-3000

Fax: 808-586-2689

Idaho Board of Nursing

www2.state.id.us/ibn

280 N. 8th Street, Suite 210

P.O. Box 83720

Boise, ID 83720

Phone: 208-334-3110

Fax: 208-334-3262

Illinois Board of Nursing

www.idfpr.com/dpr/WHO/nurs.asp

James R. Thompson Center

100 West Randolph Street, Suite 9-300

Chicago, IL 60601

Phone: 312-814-2715

Fax: 312-814-3145

Indiana State Board of Nursing

www.in.gov/pla/

Professional Licensing Agency

402 W. Washington Street,
    Room W072

Indianapolis, IN 46204

Phone: 317-234-2043

Fax: 317-233-4236

Iowa Board of Nursing

www.iowa.gov/nursing

RiverPoint Business Park

400 SW 8th Street, Suite B

Des Moines, IA 50309-4685

Phone: 515-281-3255

Fax: 515-281-4825

Kansas State Board of Nursing

www.ksbn.org

Landon State Office Building

900 S.W. Jackson, Suite 1051

Topeka, KS 66612

Phone: 785-296-4929

Fax: 785-296-3929

Kentucky Board of Nursing

www.kbn.ky.gov

312 Whittington Parkway, Suite 300

Louisville, KY 40222

Phone: 502-429-3300

Fax: 502-429-3311

**Louisiana State Board of Practical
    Nurse Examiners**

www.lsbpne.com

3421 N. Causeway Boulevard,
    Suite 505

Metairie, LA 70002

Phone: 504-838-5791

Fax: 504-838-5279

Louisiana State Board of Nursing

www.lsbn.state.la.us

17373 Perkins Road

Baton Rouge, LA 70810

Phone: 225-755-7500

Fax: 225-755-7585

Maine State Board of Nursing

www.maine.gov/boardofnursing

Mailing address:

158 State House Station

Augusta, ME 04333

Street address (for FedEx and UPS):

161 Capitol Street

Augusta, ME 04333

Phone: 207-287-1133

Fax: 207-287-1149

Maryland Board of Nursing

www.mbon.org

4140 Patterson Avenue

Baltimore, MD 21215

Phone: 410-585-1900

Fax: 410-358-3530

**Massachusetts Board of Registration
in Nursing**
www.mass.gov/dpl/boards/rn
Commonwealth of Massachusetts
239 Causeway Street, Second Floor
Boston, MA 02114
Phone: 617-973-0800
        800-414-0168
Fax: 617-973-0984

**Michigan/DCH/Bureau of Health
Professions**
www.michigan.gov/healthlicense
Ottawa Towers North
611 W. Ottawa, 1st Floor
Lansing, MI 48933
Phone: 517-335-0918
Fax: 517-373-2179

Minnesota Board of Nursing
www.nursingboard.state.mn.us
2829 University Avenue SE, Suite 200
Minneapolis, MN 55414
Phone: 612-617-2270
Fax: 612-617-2190

Mississippi Board of Nursing
www.msbn.state.ms.us
1935 Lakeland Drive, Suite B
Jackson, MS 39216-5014
Phone: 601-987-4188
Fax: 601-364-2352

Missouri State Board of Nursing
pr.mo.gov/nursing.asp
3605 Missouri Boulevard
P.O. Box 656
Jefferson City, MO 65102-0656
Phone: 573-751-0681
Fax: 573-751-0075

Montana State Board of Nursing
www.nurse.mt.gov
301 South Park, Suite 401
P.O. Box 200513
Helena, MT 59620-0513
Phone: 406-841-2345
Fax: 406-841-2305

Nebraska Board of Nursing
www.hhs.state.ne.us/crl/nursing/
        nursingindex.htm
301 Centennial Mall South
Lincoln, NE 68509-4986
Phone: 402-471-4376
Fax: 402-471-1066

**Nebraska Advanced Practice
Registered Nurse Board**
www.hhs.state.ne.us/crl/nursing/
        nursingindex.htm
301 Centennial Mall South
P.O. BOX 94986
Lincoln, NE 68509-4986
Phone: 402-471-6443
Fax: 402-471-1066

Nevada State Board of Nursing

www.nursingboard.state.nv.us

5011 Meadowood Mall Way, Suite 300

Reno, NV 89502

Phone: 775-687-7700

Fax: 775-687-7707

New Hampshire Board of Nursing

www.state.nh.us/nursing

21 South Fruit Street, Suite 16

Concord, NH 03301-2341

Phone: 603-271-2323

Fax: 603-271-6605

New Jersey Board of Nursing

www.state.nj.us/lps/ca/medical/nursing

.htm

P.O. Box 45010

124 Halsey Street, 6th Floor

Newark, NJ 07101

Phone: 973-504-6430

Fax: 973-648-3481

New Mexico Board of Nursing

www.bon.state.nm.us

6301 Indian School Road, NE,

Suite 710

Albuquerque, NM 87110

Phone: 505-841-8340

Fax: 505-841-8347

New York State Board of Nursing

www.nysed.gov/prof/nurse.htm

Education Building

89 Washington Avenue

2nd Floor West Wing

Albany, NY 12234

Phone: 518-474-3817, Ext. 280

Fax: 518-474-3706

North Carolina Board of Nursing

www.ncbon.com

3724 National Drive, Suite 201

Raleigh, NC 27602

Phone: 919-782-3211

Fax: 919-781-9461

North Dakota Board of Nursing

www.ndbon.org

919 South 7th Street, Suite 504

Bismarck, ND 58504

Phone: 701-328-9777

Fax: 701-328-9785

Northern Mariana Islands
  Commonwealth Board of Nurse
  Examiners

Mailing Address:

P.O. Box 501458

Saipan, MP 96950

Street Address (for FedEx and UPS):

#1336 Ascencion Drive

Capitol Hill

Saipan, MP 96950

Phone: 670-664-4810

Fax: 670-664-4813

Ohio Board of Nursing

www.nursing.ohio.gov

17 South High Street, Suite 400

Columbus, OH 43215-3413

Phone: 614-466-3947

Fax: 614-466-0388

Oklahoma Board of Nursing

www.youroklahoma.com/nursing

2915 N. Classen Boulevard, Suite 524

Oklahoma City, OK 73106

Phone: 405-962-1800

Fax: 405-962-1821

Oregon State Board of Nursing

www.osbn.state.or.us

17938 SW Upper Boones Ferry Road

Portland, OR 97224

Phone: 971-673-0685

Fax: 971-673-0684

Pennsylvania State Board of Nursing

www.dos.state.pa.us/bpoa/cwp/view
    .asp?a=1104&q=432869

P.O. Box 2649

Harrisburg, PA 17105-2649

Phone: 717-783-7142

Fax: 717-783-0822

**Rhode Island Board of Nurse
    Registration and Nursing
    Education**

www.health.ri.gov

105 Cannon Building

Three Capitol Hill

Providence, RI 02908

Phone: 401-222-5700

Fax: 401-222-3352

**South Carolina State Board of
    Nursing**

Mailing Address:

P.O. Box 12367

Columbia, SC 29211

Street Address:

Synergy Business Park, Kingstree
    Building

www.llr.state.sc.us/pol/nursing

110 Centerview Drive, Suite 202

Columbia, SC 29210

Phone: 803-896-4550

Fax: 803-896-4525

South Dakota Board of Nursing

www.state.sd.us/doh/nursing

4305 South Louise Avenue, Suite 201

Sioux Falls, SD 57106-3115

Phone: 605-362-2760

Fax: 605-362-2768

Tennessee State Board of Nursing

health.state.tn.us/Boards/Nursing/

index.htm

227 French Landing, Suite 300

Heritage Place MetroCenter

Nashville, TN 37243

Phone: 615-532-5166

Fax: 615-741-7899

Texas Board of Nursing

www.bon.state.tx.us

333 Guadalupe, Suite 3-460

Austin, TX 78701

Phone: 512-305-7400

Fax: 512-305-7401

Utah State Board of Nursing

www.dopl.utah.gov/licensing/nursing.html

Heber M. Wells Building, 4th Floor

160 East 300 South

Salt Lake City, UT 84111

Phone: 801-530-6628

Fax: 801-530-6511

Vermont State Board of Nursing

www.vtprofessionals.org/opr1/nurses

Office of Professional Regulation

National Life Building North F1.2

Montpelier, VT 05620-3402

Phone: 802-828-2396

Fax: 802-828-2484

Virgin Islands Board of Nurse
Licensure

www.vibnl.org

Mailing Address:

P.O. Box 304247, Veterans Drive

Station

St. Thomas, Virgin Islands 00803

Street Address (for FedEx and UPS):

#3 Kongens Gade (Government Hill)

St. Thomas, Virgin Islands 00802

Phone: 340-776-7131

Fax: 340-777-4003

Virginia Board of Nursing

www.dhp.virginia.gov/nursing

Department of Health Professions

Perimeter Center

9960 Maryland Drive, Suite 300

Richmond, VA 23233

Phone: 804-367-4515

Fax: 804-527-4455

Washington State Nursing Care
Quality Assurance Commission

fortress.wa.gov/doh/hpqa1/hps6/

Nursing/default.htm

Department of Health

HPQA #6

310 Israel Road SE

Tumwater, WA 98501-7864

Phone: 360-236-4700

Fax: 360-236-4738

West Virginia State Board of Examiners for Licensed Practical Nurses

www.lpnboard.state.wv.us

101 Dee Drive

Charleston, WV 25311

Phone: 304-558-3572

Fax: 304-558-4367

West Virginia Board of Examiners for Registered Professional Nurses

www.wvrnboard.com

101 Dee Drive

Charleston, WV 25311

Phone: 304-558-3596

Fax: 304-558-3666

Wisconsin Department of Regulation and Licensing

drl.wi.gov

Street Address:

1400 E. Washington Avenue

Madison, WI 53703

Mailing Address:

P.O. Box 8935

Madison, WI 53708-8935

Phone: 608-266-2112

Fax: 608-261-7083

Wyoming State Board of Nursing

nursing.state.wy.us

1810 Pioneer Avenue

Cheyenne, WY 82001

Phone: 307-777-7601

Fax: 307-777-3519

Appendix B

The Best Nursing Positions

BEST is a relative term. To some, best may mean high salary; to others, job satisfaction. This appendix acts as a guide to help you search for the facility that's right for you.

MAGNET HOSPITALS

Like the name implies, magnet hospitals attract nurses and other quality health care professionals. The American Nurses Credentialing Center developed the Magnet Recognition program in 1993 to recognize health-care organizations that provide nursing excellence. It is the highest level of recognition the ANCC awards to organized nursing services in the national and international healthcare communities. Nurses want to go to work and continue to work at magnet hospitals because of their desire to be associated with a healthcare facility committed to excellence in nursing. Magnet hospitals share eight essential characteristics:

1. Nurses who are clinically competent
2. Good RN-MD relationships and communication

3. Nurse autonomy and accountability

4. Supportive nurse managers, supervisors

5. Staff has input over nursing practice and practice environment

6. Support for education (in-service, continuing education, certification)

7. Adequate nurse staffing

8. Concern for the patient is paramount

What Are the Benefits of Working at a Magnet Hospital?

Magnet hospitals create a "magnet culture" with core values such as empowerment, pride, mentoring, nurturing, respect, integrity, and teamwork that provides a dynamic and positive environment for professional nurses.

Magnet hospitals give nurses a strong voice in making decisions about their work environment and patient care. You'll be supported and respected by other members of the healthcare team, including the physicians, and you will be recognized for your achievements.

Magnet hospitals offer opportunities for professional growth. You will receive support to continue your education, earn another degree, and earn certification in your nursing specialty. Magnet hospitals support your conducting research, developing evidence-based practice projects, publishing in nursing journals, and presenting at national and international conferences.

Magnet hospitals allow you to work with state-of-the-art technology, including electronic charting and bar-coded medication scanners, enabling you to spend more time at the bedside with clients and less time doing paperwork, and assisting you in providing safe care.

Magnet status contributes to overall quality care because it raises the bar for employees by establishing necessary standards.

Magnet hospitals allow you to work with other caregivers who share your dedication and passion for providing the best client care.

Where Do You Find Magnet Hospitals?

Only about 4% of hospitals have achieved magnet status. As of January 2009, 316 healthcare organizations in 43 states and the District of Columbia, as well as one in Australia and New Zealand, for their excellence in nursing service. ANCC created an easy-access website to link to each of these organizations: www.nursecredentialing.org/MagnetOrg/searchmagnet.cfm.

HIGHEST PAYING NURSING CAREERS

The following table lists the ten highest paying nursing careers, as well as the average annual salary and the educational requirements for each, according to Nurse Link (www.nursinglink.com).

Highest Paying Nursing Careers

Career	Average Annual Salary	Additional Education Required
Certified Registered Nurse Anesthetist	$135,000	Yes, Master's (MSN); Doctor of Nursing Practice (DNP) by 2015
Nurse Researcher	95,000	Yes, Doctor of Philosophy (PhD)
Psychiatric Nurse Practitioner	95,000	Yes, Master's (MSN); Doctor of Nursing Practice (DNP) by 2015
Certified Nurse Midwife	84,000	Yes, Master's (MSN); Doctor of Nursing Practice (DNP) by 2015
Pediatric Endocrinology Nurse	81,000	Variable, may need Bachelor's (BSN)
Orthopedic Nurse	81,000	Variable, may need Bachelor's (BSN)
Nurse Practitioner	78,000	Yes, Master's (MSN); Doctor of Nursing Practice (DNP) by 2015
Clinical Nurse Specialist	76,000	Yes, Master's (MSN); Doctor of Nursing Practice (DNP) by 2015
Gerontological Nurse Practitioner	75,000	Yes, Master's (MSN); Doctor of Nursing Practice (DNP) by 2015
Neonatal Nurse	74,000	Variable, may need Bachelor's (BSN)

HOTTEST NURSING SPECIALTIES

According to Nurse Link, the ten hottest nursing specialties for 2009 are:

1. Geriatric Nurse
2. Hospice and Palliative Care Nurse
3. Holistic Nurse
4. Legal Nurse Consultant
5. Correctional Nurse
6. Forensic Nurse
7. Parish Nurse (many parish nurses work as unpaid volunteers)
8. Flight Nurse
9. Psychiatric Nurse
10. Critical Care

See Chapter 6 for descriptions of nursing specialties.